FLAT

CLUES

The Sky's The Limit

By Mark Sargent

www.Booglez.com

First edition published in 2016 by Booglez Limited

Fifth Floor, 230 City Road, London

EC1V 2TT, United Kingdom

Tel: 0844 8844 622. Fax: 08712 449 500

Email: info@booglez.com

Web: www.Booglez.com

ISBN-13: 978-15238 51430

ISBN-10: 1523851430

First edition 2016

Printed and bound by Amazon Creates

NOTE: The material contained in this book is set out in good faith for general guidance and no liability can be accepted for loss or expense incurred as a result of relying in particular circumstances on statements made in this book. Laws and regulations are complex and liable to change, and readers should check the current positions with the relevant authorities in their country of origin before making personal arrangements.

This book is available online and at all good bookstores.

If using or referring to any of the material in the book, please do give credit to the author.

Contents

Acknowledgements

A massive THANK YOU to the flat earth community. Especially the pioneers who have led the way, and those individuals and groups that have been working tirelessly to help others open their mind.

Dedication

For all the truth seekers out there... your world is about to

change...

Gracias al Padre, el Hijo y el Espíritu Santo.

Preface by the Editor

The idea of the earth being flat isn't 'new' yet seems to have found a new lease of life. It is considered the monster of all "conspiracy theories" – but is it 'a theory'? Could there be some truth to this? I first heard about the notion of the earth being flat on the YouTube Radio show *Coast to Coast* and as the person being interviewed said it, I waited for the laughter... but there was none! Initially, I thought it was some sort of joke - and then I realized that he was deadly serious! This then led me to do some further research into it. One of the first videos I came across was 'Flat Earth Clues' which I found so compelling, that I told everyone I knew to watch it! From that point on, I was hooked, and have continued to tune in and consume as much material and information that I can, that is emerging on the subject.

As I began to listen in to other commentators and debaters on the topic, I noted that many would mention that the *Flat Earth Clues* was one of their first introductions to the subject of flat earth. I also noted that many You Tubers were reusing the Clues videos within their own videos because they were so powerful. Someone had taken the time to break down the crux of the topic in an easy-to-digest manner.

I was so impressed with the impact that the clues videos have had, that I followed my gut instinct to reach out to the creator of the series (Mark Sargent), to create a joint venture to use the material to create a book format for the clues. And with the help of a long time colleague (Rosie Brooks) as illustrator, the 'Flat Earth Clues' book has been created.

Do take a look at Mark's website (www.EnclosedWorld.com) and watch the clues for yourself. Tune into his radio show *Strange World* and join in the discussion.

We hope that you will take the material in the spirit in which it has been written. It's not been made necessarily to try and 'convince' you, (with an arm twisted behind your back, or a gun to your head) that we are 'right' or that 'this is it' – but we just want you to open your mind and to take a closer look at the world around you.

Question everything. And by all means - do your own research! The truth is out there! You can contact me at lisa@lisanewton.co.uk or tweet me @lisa_newton1.

Lisa Newton
Editor-in-chief
February 2016
London, UK

Your Guide To The Flat Earth

This is a readers digest version containing many of the interesting parts of the flat earth theory. For those who have already started seeing things with new eyes it will be mostly a recap but there could be a few new angles you haven't looked at. For the rest of you who are new to this the first question is invariably, is this a joke? Because it's a joke right?

And that's where we start, because it's one of our two basic childhood facts. $1 + 1 = 2$, and the earth is a globe. We're taught this before almost everything else, and that right there should give you a clue on how serious this secret is.

But for those who have forgotten their history, here's the modified "*Men In Black*" version. For the first 4,000 years of our civilization, we believed that the earth was a flatish disk, surrounded by a solid dome barrier called the Firmament. All of the five major religions had their own version of this, and the churches enforced the belief.

Then, around 1514, a man named Copernicus created a new model of the world. He stated that if the earth was spinning around 1,100 miles an hour, and circling around the sun at 60,000 miles an hour, the world was then round.

And while the math more or less worked, there was a problem. It was 1500, and the technology to prove such a theory wasn't there. The first balloon to carry people wasn't invented until 1760. Sailboats were the only travel over water, and the fastest thing on land was a horse.

But the new world view was promoted and took hold. The religions adapted to handle the new reality, and life moved on. More importantly, the globe model was quickly introduced into the education systems.

Over the next 500 years the challenges to this model faded, to the point where the globe was accepted as universally as physical laws such as gravity. **Read that again if you didn't absorb it.** For 20 generations people believed that the earth was round because there was a globe in every classroom they sat in. There was no proof.

Hundreds of years went by, and still civilization had no way of proving the theory. Planes were invented around 1900, but until 1957 nothing could go high enough to give a true perspective of where we lived.

And that's when everything got STRANGE. The United States and Russia both sent up rockets high enough to take decent pictures, and what they saw, scared them a great deal. How do we know they were extremely concerned about the sky? Because the US and Russia immediately started firing nuclear weapons straight up, and kept firing for the *next four years*.

A few things to keep in mind here. First, this was now 1958. Nuclear weapons were very expensive and hard to come by. These also weren't those nominal yield 20 kiloton toys we used on Hiroshima. This was high kiloton to low megaton, and we couldn't get them up fast enough....

And the strangeness continued in other places. In 1959, only a year into the atmosphere bombardment, 10 nations including the US made Antarctica off limits to any colonization. A treaty was put in place and to this day remains intact. Over 50 nations now have signed off on this treaty.

Do you know any treaty that has lasted that long between all industrialized nations? More over, do you know any piece of real estate in the world that is owned by no one? You would think at the very least one of the large oil companies would use their huge financial resources to explore this region, and yet they don't even petition the idea.

The short version of the discovery is this. By 1958 the military had discovered the very solid upper and outer edges of our world, and had to create a way to put up "do not enter" signs without looking obvious. It was tricky, but if there is one thing that I have learned about the authority, it's that nothing is left to chance.

Most of the work had already been done for them, so their job was primarily in the details. The sky part of the dome was much higher than commercial air traffic, so the only thing they had to worry about there was the space program, which was immediately militarized. The outer border had the natural benefit of not only an extensive ocean, but a scaling decrease in temperature, and a steady increase in iceberg frequency to discourage ships, all leading to a permanently frozen land mass that could not be used for any form of agriculture.

This ocean and ice layout had worked well for thousands of years, because the technology of the current civilization didn't evolve quickly. Sailors avoided cold weather seas whenever possible, and oxygen levels get low enough to harm people even on high mountains.

The brilliance of the design comes in the simple fact that human males are corrupted by power. Corruption so total in fact that they would rather hide the world itself rather than risk their power on it. You could theorize that Kings and Popes were told of the world a long time ago. Maybe an ancient scroll or book. Perhaps an inter dimensional being told the tale of what the world looked like, but this was all but dismissed because even the most powerful leaders of the day couldn't reach the borders, and if they couldn't, what chance did the general public have?

It's one thing to be told of the giant, impenetrable dome, but it's a whole different animal when you finally stand right next to it. Then the tough decisions have to be made. Do we keep the secret, and how far are we willing to go to keep the status quo?

Once they decided to keep the secret, no expense was spared. The rapid progression of rocketry science had to be addressed quickly, and so the Moon missions were created.

Matt from the NASA Channel was right in his thinking that you needed the moon mission event to stage a picture of the earth from deep orbit, and that couldn't be more true. Establishing NASA as the front runner of space exploration also diverted people who would have otherwise created their own space companies for profit.

The best engineers, technicians, and pilots were recruited to the NASA space program. Once there, they were compartmentalized on a need to know basis. The astronauts know of the deception, and are sworn to secrecy under the penalty of whatever motivates them.

Private space programs are discouraged, sabotaged, or absorbed into the NASA fold. Private sector space craft are just not going to be allowed for several reasons; the most obvious is the collision with the dome itself. The telemetry data from such a mission would show an impact failure at a certain altitude, and if repeated, would raise questions NASA just isn't prepared to answer.

There are three perpetual questions about our world that can't be eliminated, but avoided at all costs. These are the questions you should ask yourself and others, if this protective layer is going to be lifted.

1. I'd like to preface this with a thank you to Max Malone, a conspiracy hard core who has a knack for boiling down debates to a single paragraph whenever possible. After over 50 years and thousands of hours of space travel footage, both by NASA and other countries, is there no exterior shot where the astronaut completes the simple act of panning the camera 180 degrees, let along a full 360 sweep.

No moon mission, exterior space station, nothing, **ever**. Statistics will tell you that this would have already happened by accident years ago, but it hasn't, and it won't. This is because of the rule they cannot break, the same rule that applies to television set shows that never show the fourth wall. Why? **There is no fourth wall**.

2. When you search online for pictures of the earth from space, 95% of what you will see is a collection of artificial composite shots. In 2000 when I did this search there was exactly one picture by NASA, showing the bottom part of Africa and Antarctica. Now that picture is hidden within hundreds of simulated images. There are HD cameras everywhere and no one is taking a shot of the earth, because you can't get enough altitude to do it.

3. The commercial air travel routes for the Southern hemisphere are wrong. This is an easy thing you can check out in 60 seconds. Take a map reading of the distance between anywhere near Australia and anywhere in South America. It's a straight shot across the South Pacific. Now find your favorite

travel site and try to get there non-stop. See what happens. The routes start turning ridiculous. I used to business travel for years, and I've never seen anything like it.

It's the one thing in the general public world they can't hide, the actual distance between these two places. On a round world the flight is easy, just a straight shot across an ocean, but on a flat world, it becomes the greatest distance between two points. There are no shortcuts, so they distract you with multiple connects and layovers. It's only blind luck that the United States was in the Northern hemisphere; otherwise the increased traffic would have raised eyebrows by now.

I know, I know, its madness, its lunacy. There are people who will tell you straight to your face that all the leaders of the world are Lizards, and yet laugh out loud when you say the words flat earth.

I was, and still am, a huge conspiracy guy. I literally ran out of new tin hat topics to research and I STILL wouldn't look at this one without embarrassment, but every time I glanced at it there was something unresolved, and once I saw the near perfection of the whole plan, I was hooked.

Do your own homework, ask the questions, get past the possibility and see if you can move into an even bigger picture, like who built the dome, and why. That's where it starts to get really interesting, and things start opening up.

I know I said years ago that the greater good was something that should be preserved, that JFK, Pearl Harbor, and 911 were inevitable, I still believe it, and I understand the decisions. The globe illusion however has run its course over the last 500 years, time to start again. If that means we end up getting the attention of who or what created this place, and force the reset of the world, is that such a bad thing?

I've included some website links in the resources section that you might want to check out, like the current map projections used by the USGS, the United Nations logo, the flat earth society, high altitude nuclear tests, the Antarctica treaty, among others.

Initially I didn't allow ratings or comments on the videos for several reasons. One, this topic seems to bring out the worst debates because of the initial denial, that and I've seen dedicated trolls on the flat earth society website who show up every day and say the same thing to new forum members. It's a joke; it's not serious, nothing to see here. Kind of strange that there are full time trolls on a site that has less than 500 members worldwide eh?

That being said, please feel free to email me at msargent23@comcast.net or heck just call 303-494-6631, I know no one uses the actual phone anymore but I'll answer what I can....

Clue 1
The Empty Theatre

This is part of a series of clues that can help you get your head around both the design of the flat earth system we live in, and who has been involved in the deception to hide it from you.

The clue you have to look at is built upon another conspiracy that has been around for decades, namely the space program. Most of those watching this are aware of the varying theories revolving around NASA, the Apollo program, the space shuttle, the international space station, and so on.

The clue itself isn't based on one of these highly debated topics, but the lack of one, more specifically, motion pictures based on actual events.

This, like others in the series, is something you can check out for yourself. Everything you need to reference this is online. To begin, think of all the movies involving space travel that you've seen in your lifetime.

You'll start with the obvious, *Star Wars, Star Trek, Alien*, just to name a few. In fact if you go through your own personal list, you could probably come up with over 100 different off world movies without breaking much of a sweat. This part is easy.

For the second group, try to come up with space movies that aren't fantasy based. You'll get a list that has *Red Planet, Gravity, Mission to Mars, 2001,* things like that. These films will usually take on a not so distant future theme and where we could be down the road, and it's still a pretty good sized list.

These first two groups of films are encouraged by the authority, because they reinforce the globe model view through assumption. The entertainment system demands that the globe view and solar system concept is a given, therefore, the actual world view must also be true.

Or to put it another way, if you are using your suspension of disbelief as you watch a movie like, say, *Gravity*, then subconsciously you are reinforcing the movie right on top of the real world.

The more of these movies you watch and enjoy, the more the lines blur between what you want to believe and what you actually know. Watch enough movies about Mars, and you will be less astonished when NASA announces an actual mission to Mars. Same with the moon, other solar systems, and so on.

Releasing the movie "*2001, a Space Odyssey*" in 1968, right before the actual moon missions, was no accident. It took the greatest director of the time 5 years to make and several people who saw the theatre screenings claim that many military groups were listed in the credits, only to be removed years later.

But 2001 is just a side note of this clue. For those who really want to dig into Stanley Kubrick's hidden vision, I highly recommend the documentary "*Room 237*"[1]. A link to it is below, and also in the resources section at the end.

Now you are aware of the first two groups of space films. There are those that contain generous amounts of fantasy, and those who try to paint our near future. These two groups are easy to find.

The third group is the challenge, and again, that's where things get interesting. The moon missions concluded in 1972, and even though it's still considered the greatest achievement by mankind, no fact based movies were made regarding it until "*The Right Stuff*" was released in 1983. Now you might

---

[1] Room 237 documentary - http://en.wikipedia.org/wiki/Room_237

say that it had only been 11 years and maybe it was tough to get the rights, and so on, but that's not what made the film interesting.

The movie ran extremely long for 1983, coming in at three hours and 12 minutes. It was an exhaustive look at the astronaut selection process, the competition, and the training facility itself, but when the credits rolled thee hours later, chronologically, they had only gotten to the low earth orbit missions. Just for fun, Google the right stuff movie and see how many spacecraft you can find.

It won four academy awards, and did a great job at the box office, but the Apollo missions were never touched.

The only other major motion picture that involved the actual moon program was *Apollo 13* in 1995, a full 12 years later. Apollo 13 only covered a single moon orbit, with no landing or close up reference to the previous missions below them. And after 1995, that was it. Nothing.

Hollywood is known for leaving no stone unturned with reboots and sequels to nearly everything, yet in almost 60 years, there has never been a single moon mission movie based on actual events. Hundreds of science fiction films referencing it, everything from Superman to the Transformers, but literally nothing that covers the moon surface. Six complete moon missions involving multiple vehicles, moon buggies, playing golf, and no one wants to touch it.

Now to be fair, there was a TV miniseries in 1998 covering the subject. It was produced by Tom Hanks who got involved after starring in Apollo 13. There has been no professional production of any kind since then. Again, just for fun, Google from earth to the moon TV series and see what you find.

The why is easy, and the clue revealed. If Hollywood makes a movie about the moon landings, and it's indistinguishable from the real thing, then how do you know which is real? It raises some subtle questions involving stage technique, and how long they have been in place. If Hollywood could fake it now, then when did they first have the ability?

There is one other movie which stands out, and I mention it because I can't believe it ever got made. It is *Capricorn One*. The film's plot involved the faking of a Mar's mission and how it could be accomplished. In short, it's part of the conspiracy world bible. I highly recommend it and the link is below[2] (and also in the resources section).

To summarize, all space movies are encouraged by the authority, except for the ones that are based on actual accounts. Those are not allowed. The moon program has been buried in entertainment because the moon cannot be reached. It's either outside the barrier, or just a highly rendered image, like any planet you see when entering a video game. The world is FLAT, and this is just one clue.

So do some of your own research, and ask questions!

---

[2] Capricorn One 1978 movie - http://en.wikipedia.org/wiki/Capricorn_One

Clue 2

Byrd Wall

This clue revolves around one of the most remarkable men you may have never heard of, **Richard E. Byrd** and his relationship with Antarctica, and the secretive missions he carried out there until his dying day.

Some of you have followed the legend of Richard Byrd through the hollow earth theory. We aren't going to be covering any hollow earth in this chapter, but instead focus on the man and his involvement with the South Pole.

The readers digest version of Richard Byrd is as follows: Born in 1888, he became an American naval officer who specialized in feats of exploration. He was a pioneering American aviator, Medal of Honor winner, polar explorer, aircraft navigator, expedition leader in the worst environments in the world, and the youngest Admiral in the history of the navy.

In addition, his list of awards takes up several pages in Wikipedia, including three ticker tape parades in his honor. In short, he was Indiana Jones on steroids. Some people will say that Roy Chapman Andrews was the real Indiana Jones, and you might be right, but Richard Byrd beat Indy six days a week and twice on Sunday.

I mention all his accolades to paint a picture of credibility and trust. The governments of the US and the world trusted his judgment and leadership, and they took advantage of every chance they had to put him in charge of special missions.

The first large scale mission was an expedition to Antarctica in 1928. This was noteworthy because even though he had just flown over the North Pole in 1926, all expeditions from 1928 on were focused on the South. The expedition lasted two years, and during it, at the age of 41, was promoted to Admiral.

His second Antarctic expedition ran from 1933 to 1935, and his third from 1939 to 1940. While in Antarctica he also was an advisor for other countries who had their own expeditions, including England, France, Germany, and building off previous countries expeditions from Belgium, Japan and Sweden.

He then helped lead US Navy fleet operations in World War 2, was present during the Japanese surrender in 1945, but then something strange happened....He went back to Antarctica.

Now some of you aren't surprised, because he'd been there since 1928, and I agree with you, it's the *how* that's interesting here.

His fourth trip to Antarctica wasn't an expedition, it was a military operation called Operation "*High Jump*".

Commanding an entire aircraft carrier group that included 13 support ships, Admiral Byrd led 4,700 men to the South Pole, for reasons that are still shrouded to this day.

Some say they were chasing the remaining Nazi fleet, even though Germany had surrendered a full year earlier. Others say that there was a Nazi base established in Antarctica during the war, when Admiral Byrd was absent. None of these theories are important for this clue.

What we do know is that the US had sent an excessively large military force to the ice, all under the guise of peaceful intentions.

During this operation, Admiral Byrd told a Chile newspaper this:

The most important result of his observations and discoveries is the potential effect that they have in relation to the security of the United States. The fantastic speed with which the world is shrinking – recalled the admiral – is one of the most important lessons learned during his recent Antarctic exploration. I have to warn my compatriots that the time has ended when we were able to take refuge in our isolation and rely on the certainty that the distances, the oceans, and the poles were a guarantee of safety.

After the operation, Admiral Byrd toured the states, and gave interviews. The most interesting of which as a national television show in 1954 called the Longines Chronoscope, a horrible name, but a decent show. I've added the transcript to the end of this chapter and put the reference link below[3] and in the resources, so that you can watch it for yourself.

During this television interview, he first spoke of an area beyond the South Pole as large as the United States, which no one had set foot on yet. He then went on to say that there would probably be expeditions year after year because the US government had really become interested.

The interviewers then probed as to why the interest in the South, when any perceived military threat from Russia (keep in mind this was 1954) would be from the North. He went on to say that it was the most valuable and important place in the

___

[3] US Television interview with Admiral Richard Byrd, 1954 - https://www.youtube.com/watch?v=czW0iRJuH1A

world for science. It involved the future of the nation, an untouched reservoir of untapped resources, including coal, oil, minerals, and uranium.

He added that at the time of this interview, there were seven nations currently engaged in Antarctica including Russia, Australia, Argentina, Chile, and New Zealand.

During the interview the Admiral talked about planning the next military mission to Antarctica. It was called Operation Deep Freeze, and ran from 1955 to 1956.

The mission was completed, and he supposedly returned home.

Now this is where you come in and say, so what, and normally I'd agree with you, except for what happened next. Nothing happened next. The missions just **suddenly stopped**, and that was it! No other expeditions, military or otherwise were conducted on the continent, **ever**!

Then a treaty was put in place banning any country from doing basically anything. **The end.**

And if you're wondering what you're missing, it's this: Admiral Byrd goes on television, says that this massive body of land, most of which sits on a plateau 2 miles high, is rich with every resource you could ever want, ENERGY rich, pristine, with no indigenous population or plant life, and every country that has sent teams is ready to carve it up like a big turkey, not to mention there's a expanse of land larger than the United States they haven't even LOOKED at yet, and out of the blue everyone just calls the whole thing off? There are no environmentalists in 1959; this is the land of Diner food and 20 cent gas!

I'm calling total BS on this one. The dollar value of the initial resource find would have fueled armies of greedy companies. So what happened? They found the edge that's what, and the last thing they were going to do was let unsupervised companies near it, regardless of the money. Even if hundreds of miles away, you couldn't allow resource corporations even into a safe area, and then years down the road as they expanded, tell them, oh, sorry, you can't go beyond this point. When the companies ask why, what would they tell them?

And now the interior of Antarctica is off limits, with no revisions until the year 2041. You can take tours of the outer islands, but there is a hidden line, enforced by the military, that you will not be able to cross.

Because the interior is actually the exterior edge. It's there, it's hidden, and it's protected.

The earth you live on is flat.

So do some of your own research, and ask questions.

Transcript – Admiral Byrd interview

I – Interviewer (Frank Knight)

AB – Admiral Byrd

I: Our very distinguished guest for this evening, is Admiral Richard E Byrd. The North Pole used to be a no mans land, but these are the days when, by buying a ticket on a commercial airliner, you can fly across the North Pole and drink a cocktail at the same time. In only three score or more years ago, about 35 years ago, our guest tonight, found out whether there was any land north of the North American continent. He made that first discovery flight, and I must say that Admiral Byrd, our guest tonight, is not only our greatest living explorer, but he's been an inspiration to countless Americans.

Admiral Byrd, you've been to both the North Pole and the South Pole. Is there any unexplored land left on this earth that might appeal to adventurous young Americans?

AB: Yes, there is. Not up around the North pole because it's getting crowded up there now because they're finding out its really useable, not only to live in, but militarily. But strangely enough, there's left in the world today, an area as big as the United States, that's never been seen by human beings, and that's beyond the pole on the other side of the South pole, from middle America.

And I think it's quite astonishing, that there should be an area as big as that, unexplored, so there's a lot of adventure left down at the bottom of the world.

I: Admiral, an expedition to which you are the advisor is now en route, what is that expedition doing?

AB: Well, that's the icebreaker "Adtka", and it's a reconnaissance expedition that's going down to the South Pole area to make certain observations, and look for some bases. They will be back in April, and report back, and upon the information we get from that undertaking, we will base the bigger expedition that is to follow.

I: Is that very definitely planned?

AB: That is being planned right now. So I'm willing to say to you that there will be a number of expeditions that will follow year after year at the bottom of the world, because the government has really become interested.

I: Well Admiral Byrd I can understand how everyone is interested in the North pole, because it's so near our greatest challenger, Soviet Russia. But why this interest in the bottom of the world. Nobody lives down there, is there?
AB: No, it's pretty cold. There is only one permanent resident, and that's the emperor penguin, the little ones live further north.

I'll tell you one reason they are interested, it's by far the most important and valuable place left in the world for science. That's where the scientific groups from all over the world are interested.

But more important than that, it has to do with the future of the nation, and those to come after us, even during your lifetime, because it happens to be an untouched reservoir of natural resources, and as the world shrinks with ever increasing acceleration, far flung places which we used to think were useless, like the North pole, and no mans land, become very useful. The bottom of the world, will be important, not only to us, but to our allies.

I: I was going to ask you, does it have military importance?

AB: It has some. Now as the world shrinks, it will continue to shrink with ever increasing acceleration, thus bringing these places closer, and in the future, and I can see a time when it will become very very important strategically.

I: Has the development of air power increased the strategic importance of places like the South Pole?

AB: Very much so, very much so. Even now, if anything happened, and we lost the Panama Canal, we would have to control the islands just North of Antarctica, which are a part, of Antarctica.

I: Admiral you speak of the resources of Antarctica, what are they? What are the natural resources there?

AB: Well, we've found enough coal within 180 miles of the South Pole, in a great ridge of mountains that's not covered in snow, enough to supply to whole world for quite a while. That's the coal, now there is evidence of many other minerals, we're pretty sure there is oil, that coal shows the bottom of the world, now by far the coldest spot in the world where that coal is, gets to 100 below zero in the winter. It was once tropical. So we think there is oil there, and there is evidence, probably uranium.

I: Is it any secret, is there uranium there that would be the only thing practical to actually go after I suppose. Everything else would be economically unfeasible wouldn't it?

AB: Well, as we recklessly expend our resources, the time will come, when we'll have to go after that stuff down there. You know I avoided what you said about uranium, I'm not sure; I don't want to fight over the Antarctic.

I: Is there a competition among other nations as to trying to get information about Antarctica and to possibly secure some of these resources?

AB: Well, yes. There are now several nations very much interested. Russia is interested tremendously that I am sure. Australia has an expedition down there, the Argentines, Chile,

New Zealand, Britain, and so on. Now you can understand those people being interested because they live down there, the New Zealanders, the Argentines, the Chileans, and the Australians, and so, we don't do much about claiming anything.

I: Admiral, you make it sound crowded. Are there that many Expeditions down there or in route there?

AB: Well you know, as I said, it's the most peaceful place in the world, but I don't think it will be for long because of this intense interest on the part of other nations and this nation.

Clue 3
Map Makers

This clue looks into the USGS, otherwise known as the map makers of the world, and a few surprising things that they and others have in common with the flat earth idea.

All the reference links are provided either in footnotes to the page, or in the resources section at the end of the book, and I encourage you to check them out.

For those of you outside of the United States, USGS stands for United States Geological Survey, a scientific branch of the US Government. Formed in 1879, and with the help of the ever expanding American Empire, they quickly became the premier map makers of the known world. Currently, they have around 9,000 employees and an annual budget of over a billion dollars a year.

They also have extensive science departments covering biology, geography, geology, hydrology and many programs tied to them. Their motto since the 1990's has been "science for a changing world", and I'm going to show you how true that really is.

What does this large, really boring government group have to do with the flat earth? To understand that you have to look into their origins, which is in geography. To do this you'll need to look at a source that specializes in maps. There are maps you can see in Wikipedia, but there are others you can reference as well.

The Wiki list of map projections[4] isn't much to look at as a whole, although there a number of interesting takes on the world view. Not only do they have just about every perspective when it comes to the land we live on, but some detailed information on where the map originated, including name type, the origin or creator, and the year the map perspective was proposed.

Now some of these will be very familiar, especially the ones that you would see on your classroom wall. There are a

---

[4] https://en.wikipedia.org/wiki/List_of_map_projections

number of variations here, but the one that has been debated on recently would be this one, the Gall Peters, which accurately shows the size difference between the continents, the most obvious clue being that the white continent of Greenland is actually tiny compared to Africa. But I digress.

If you keep going down through all the different shapes, you'll get into circular maps, but only one of these is a top down perspective that shows the continents in the center, surrounded by an unbroken ring of ice. In Wiki, it's called the Azimuthal Equidistant[5], and just to make it easier I'm going to abbreviate and call it AE for short. The AE Map is below:

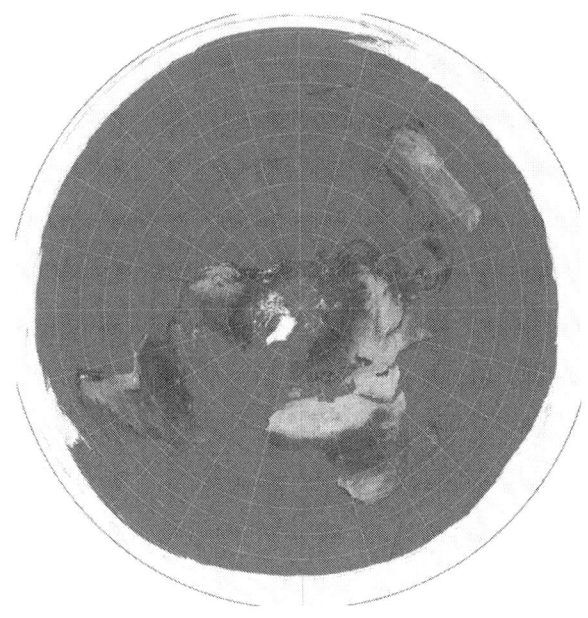

5

https://en.wikipedia.org/wiki/List_of_map_projections#/media/File:Azimuthal _equidistant_projection_SW.jpg

Why is this map so interesting? Well if you're looking at the Wiki page you'll spot a few reasons. The first is that in the notes section this map. And I quote "*Used by the USGS in the National Atlas of the US*". It also mentions that it is used as the emblem of the United Nations. Of all the maps on this screen, it is the only one that references a group of any kind.

And if you keep this page open and navigate over to the flat earth section of Wiki, you'll notice towards the bottom of the page a similar map. I've referenced it here and you can tell quite easily it's identical, but not referenced or linked as the AE model.

To make things even stranger, we go back to the USGS model and you see that it was first proposed 1000 years ago and you may think, well, that's a bad link, so you compare it with the person who proposed it and you get this guy, **Al Biruni**. Who was Al Biruni? Well he lived around 1000 years ago and was considered one of the greatest scholars of his era, schooled in multiple sciences.

Have you ever heard of him? I hadn't. Maybe it's multiple bad references in Wiki. Well no, because NASA knows who he is and named this moon crater after him. So why is the USGS using a version of the world map designed by a 1000 year old Persian scientist? Because it's correct, that's why.

So to be clear, let's compare them again, the United Nations flag, the USGS official map of the earth, and the flat earth model. All identical, but one isn't recognized and instead ridiculed as an outdated look at the world.

And this is one of those political quandaries that the authority gets stuck in. The short version is this. The government is on the same page as the flat earth, but they can't admit it, even in confidence. We know the earth isn't flat, "but it really is". We know you use the same map as we do, but ours is just an image, and anyone who says differently is obviously crazy.

Makes you wonder how long the USGS had been using that model as an official reference. The UN started using it for their logos in 1945, and then made some final adjustments in 1946. And the UN flag also raises a few questions like, why isn't Antarctica represented on the map? Is it supposed to be assumed in the outer circle, or perhaps the spiky olive branches on the outside? They don't mention it anywhere online.

Flag of the United Nations[6]

---

[6] https://en.wikipedia.org/wiki/Flag_of_the_United_Nations

This is what I like to focus on, the gaps, the holes in the plot, the unanswered questions. The USGS using the same map as the flat earth, but not saying why, not recognizing it, or that you can't link the very same image from the flat earth Wiki back to the actual AE definition of the projection.

The authority figured out in the 1950's all of the borders of our enclosed world, and have done a great job hiding it over the decades. But the world's a complex place, and there are clues out there just lying around. I think it's time you saw some of them.

So do some of your own research, and ask questions.

Clue 4
Shell Beach

This clue covers the near perfect design of the flat earth model and will break down some of the logic behind the decisions made. It sounds like a big task, and it is, but to start, let's look at something small, like this little guy (above).

Take an ordinary mouse, and put it into a glass cage. It doesn't have to be a mouse, it could be a snake, a lizard, an insect - it makes little difference for this exercise. People identify with mice because they're used to seeing them in lab experiments. Mice also don't have any sinister connotations. They're seen as relatively innocent and benign, the perfect test subjects as it were. I have yet to meet anyone who has a bias against the lab mouse.

So the mouse goes into the box for the first time, and the reaction is always the same. It explores its surroundings, and more importantly, tests the barrier around it, probing for exits, or potential exits.

The mouse inspects every inch of its new glass home, and at some point, settles into the acceptance that the walls are indeed solid and that it may be there a while. Every so often, it will repeat the process, again checking the boundaries of the cage, just in case something had changed.

What it doesn't do, is act like it would in the wild, because it realizes that it's in a form of captivity. The glass box doesn't even remotely resemble its natural environment. You could put this box in the middle of the forest and the mouse may feel slightly better about its situation, but it still knows that it's been trapped against its will, and will settle into a non-native lifestyle.

You could take all the other small animals that could be substituted for a mouse, the snake, the lizard, the insect, it makes no difference, the result will invariably be the same, repeated probing for escape routes, then acceptance.

Take the same animal, and now put it into the middle of a 100 mile square wildlife preserve, surrounded on all sides by a similar type of glass enclosure. The creature doesn't even bother to rush to the sides of the preserve and start testing the boundaries, mostly because it is out of visual range.

It could be days, or even weeks before it even encounters a single fence. The animals' routine is spent doing what it normally would do. It eats, it sleeps, and it breeds. It does everything that it would naturally do in the wild. If one day the animal approaches the fence, there might be some curiosity, but any anxiety is quickly resolved by just turning around and heading back into the vast expanse from which it came.

The fence does not pose a potential problem for the animals in the preserve, because it is so small compared to the expanse they live in, and dwelling on it doesn't hold any interest. We're assuming here that the fence is high enough to discourage flying creatures as well, deep enough to stop burrowing classes, and if you want, reaches the floor of any nearby bodies of water, stopping any clever aquatic types.

The point here is that all creatures great and small, inside a giant wildlife preserve, when encountering the fence, wouldn't care. They would all in their own way, just shrug and move on with their lives.

However, if you take a human, male or female, regardless of education or nurturing, and put them in the exact same wildlife sanctuary, the response would be quite different. When the human approaches the glass fence, they don't see it as a minor distraction. They pause, they wonder, and more importantly, they ask questions, either internally or amongst others.

Why is this fence here? How far does it reach? Can I dig underneath, or climb over, or go around it? These questions continue in the way you might imagine, but eventually, a bigger question jumps to the top of the list; who built the fence?

It is this that which changes not only the type of questions being asked, but how the human being (or beings) look at their world. The giant wildlife preserve suddenly gets smaller. Each new fence border discovered starts to artificially constrict the expanse, even though the dimensions haven't changed.

Before long, the preserve, their home, loses some of its relevance. The fence is a reminder of the unknown. It provokes fear and endless speculation within the human. Given enough time, the importance of the preserve continues to be reduced, especially in relation to the fence, and the reason why it's so engrossing for the human is simple; it's THERE. It's real. They can see it, and maybe even touch it.

Adding more humans to the equation increases the disparity of the situation by orders or magnitude. Have you seen the fence? Do you know how long it's been here? Have you ever known anyone that's been outside it? It's older than us. Who is responsible for the fence? What can we do to appease the group that created it? You can see what this might lead to.

A long lasting group hysteria would entrench itself within the population, grab hold and never let go. The fence is bigger, older, and wiser than they are. It humbles them, it angers them, and it is forever. It is their proof of a higher power. Maybe not God, but certainly "God-like".

No civilization, regardless of technology, discipline, or age, would be able to cope with the existence of it. For the human psyche, there are just too many questions that go unanswered. Life would never be able to progress normally.

To summarize, a garden variety wildlife preserve would work for 99.99 percent of all the worlds' life forms. For human beings however, you would need to make some modifications, or really just one big one.

So let's take a look at a few examples of how this could be accomplished, and from there expand it. The first failed example can be seen in the 1998 movie "Dark City[7]". This is a good starting point to get you in the right mindset. The premise here is that an advanced race creates a small flat earth area, complete with the traditional dome. The design however is initially flawed, in that they built the city all the way to the outer edge, leaving no room for error.

To compensate for this, they altered the memories of the human population on a regular basis, therefore repressing any long term investigations. However in movies there are always

---

[7] http://en.wikipedia.org/wiki/Dark_City_(1998_film)

anomalies, like the police officer who realizes that even though he remembers visiting a place called shell beach, there is no way to reach it, because shell beach is outside the flat world, and never existed. He just keeps going around the circular city that has no exits. In the end another man, the hero of the movie, makes it to edge, steals the advanced races power, and creates an ocean, which really should have been there in the first place.

Move from there to a movie released only four months later called "*Truman Show*[8]". Inevitably all flat earthers have to take a hard look at this movie from a technical point of view. The movie follows the same type of lines as *Dark City*, but in a much more relatable premise, that of a giant television stage built so that the outside world can watch a person go through his life without any knowledge that he is living inside a flat world, surrounded by a physical dome.

This movie is interesting on several levels, including construction. Using their existing model of a small town bordered on one side by a large lagoon and wilderness, and the other a seemingly expansive ocean, while better than *Dark City*, still had its flaws. For one, it was less than 20 miles across, and even though Truman's desire to explore was repressed, there was still a chance that he would venture to the outer edge, which is where the movie ended.

---

[8] https://en.wikipedia.org/wiki/The_Truman_Show

But for the most part, it worked. Truman believed the entire scenario because he was born into it and then lived 30+ years without any reason to doubt where he was, which could be said for any of us. If it wasn't for the "and we'll say movie mistakes" that the studio fell victim to, then the show would have never ended.

And this then raises hypothetical scenarios, like, how many kids like Truman could you have raised inside that dome? 10? 50? Now logistically you can see how it might be problematic in keeping tabs on that may kids, especially as they got older, but with enough slight of hand, it could be possible.

A fictional situation just like that was made into the 2004 movie "The Village[9]", and even though it turned into one of those M Night Shyamalan plot twist things, the premise was very feasible. A wealthy group of idealists buy a large parcel of land in an existing wildlife preserve, create a small town from the 1800's, and raise children there. They pay off government officials to keep planes far away, and spread a myth that monsters live in the forest.

As far as the kids are concerned, they actually are living in a small Pennsylvania town in the 1800's, and being born into it, why wouldn't they? If the story continued, eventually the elders that founded the town would all pass away, leaving the children to pass on the legacy, free from any burden of guilt that their world was not what it appeared to be.

---

[9] https://en.wikipedia.org/wiki/The_Village_(2004_film)

And keep in mind this was done with very little land manipulation and NO DOME.

This then circles back to how many actors the fictional Truman show really needed to hire. Other than the leads who did product placement, the rest of the town could actually just live their lives like anyone else, use phone lines to call outside, go to restaurants, watch television at home, and so on. But again, I digress.

Assuming the technology was possible, how many people like Truman could you keep in a dome the size of say, a state? Hundreds of miles across? Probably thousands. If you kept expanding the size of the dome to a few thousand miles, well then you're talking millions, but when it gets that big, something interesting happens. You don't need the actors anymore. Start it up like the Village, and within just a few generations, everyone is oblivious, and you can leave them to their own devices. Starting to sound familiar?

In fact, the larger you make the enclosed world, the less micro managing needs to be done. It gets easier as it scales. This brings us back to the missing modification you need for the human race. To keep the storylines consistent, and remove all the hocus pocus of monsters in the woods, or that you can't get to Shell Beach, you place in gradual negative reinforcement, one that creates an illusion of choice.

Say for example that Truman went out in the sailboat the same as before, but this time the dome was twice the size, and the simulated ocean far larger. How far would he travel before getting hungry, thirsty, or tired? The movie ending is then in doubt.

And if you compare this scenario with where you are now, then you start to see it. Look at the flat earth map again. Continents grouped in the center, surrounded in all directions by hundreds of miles of SALT water. Think about how much farther ancient ships would have traveled if you could drink what you were sailing on. As you move closer to the edge the temperature starts taking a nose dive, and then you start seeing icebergs. If that doesn't stop you then you run into what we call Antarctica, which is a steep climb two miles up, with no plant life or indigenous livestock animals.

And if you had the where with all to make it that far, you would still have hundreds of miles of endless ice and snow. It's easy to see why so few people have gone the distance.

Compare this to the upper ceiling, which is much easier to maintain. You simply decrease the oxygen rates so that every 1000 feet up it gets more difficult to breathe. This slows down exploration over mountains ranges, and discourages limited control flight, such as balloons. Also keep in mind that the dome itself doesn't have to be that high in relation to the outer ring. With commercial aircraft capping out at 10 miles, and rockets less than 400, the dome would actually look more

49

like stadium roof, depending on how you wanted to display things like the sun, moon, and stars.

An enclosed world with these types of safeguards would be able to sustain an unknowing population for say what, 4500 years? Then you artificially introduce a globe model into the scientific community before the civilization technology reaches a point that could lead to discovery.

And 500 years later, here we are. A civilization inside an amazing structure, doing what we would naturally do, while the authority stands by the gate and fears the consequences if we ever found out for ourselves.

So do some of your own research, and ask questions.

Clue 5
Status Quo

This clue covers the inevitable and sometimes frustrating question of why the authority would go to all the trouble of hiding the flat earth. My hope here is to show you different angles, and a progression of events, all of which lead to a very changed world, both physically, and mentally.

To open we have to go way back to when the world was a much simpler place. You had your five major religions including Buddhism, Hinduism, Judaism, Islam, and Christianity. Each of these groups had their own version of what is known in Genesis as **the firmament**, or a flat, circular world enclosed by a solid dome like barrier from where the creator (or creators) looked on.

51

I'm not going to explore all the subtle differences between the groups, suffice it to say that it's interesting that despite their differences that led to acts of horrible violence between them, there was no real earth model debate.

So then around 500 years ago, the science community, led by Copernicus who probably had a little help, introduced what we now know as the heliocentric, or globe model of the world, which in turn changed the solar system, galaxy, and so on.

The religions, seeing that this globe model was gaining popularity, feared a loss in the fan base, so they all adapted their religions to include the globe model. From their point of view, it was a small change from a circular to a globe world, and really, in a few generations who would remember anyway?

So the churches, mosques, temples wrapped up their flat earth model in metaphoric soft cloth, and put it in the drawer with the good silver for safe keeping. Remember this because we'll come back to it later.

And hundreds of years went by, with science promoting all the aspects of the globe, and the religions promoting their beliefs upon this globe. The world kept spinning, so to speak, and everyone was happy.

Then in the early part of the 1900's you get this pesky explorer named Richard Byrd. He has family money, all the right connections, and secures basically unlimited funding and the government green light to probe every piece of unseen territory there is. It was inevitable I guess, a young man who has an unquenchable desire to see all that there is to see, and then granting him the tools needed to accomplish this goal.

And he pulls a Truman and gets lucky, crossing the vast salt ocean, avoiding the icebergs, arriving at the frozen coastline, and he keeps going. He was never going to stop. One day after crossing hundreds of miles of high altitude ice and snow, Admiral Byrd sees it. **A barrier.**

And to him, it is just A barrier, not **THE** barrier. He is but a tiny spec in front of it. It stretches out on both sides as far as he can see, and straight up so far that he can't discover the beginning of the arc. The great explorer now has a new challenge, finding the shape of this thing. It's much like a blind man describing an elephant. Until you feel out the whole thing, what do you really know?

If you look at the AE or Flat Earth overhead map, you see the problem. To even determine the scope of the outer wall, you have to circle it. It would have taken months, if not years. You could use a series of ships going in opposite directions, or planes, but there are refueling stations that need to be built and so on. His task was challenging to say the least. Admiral Byrd kept laying the groundwork of the great discovery until his eventual death in 1957.

A year later, the United States and Russia found the upper edge. From there, the math was easy, and moreover, you could actually see the real world. Then of course there is the decision, or deception, depending on how you looked at it. The authority made the call to hide the actual shape of where we live, then sealed off the outer edge from prying eyes, and created the space program to not only reinforce the globe model, but to control it.

There was really only one reason they cared about this, and it takes a while to process, so let's look at the immediate effects of actual disclosure, and work our way up to the authority's biggest fear.

For this exercise we'll look at releasing the news today, instead of say 1958. While 1958 would have been easier, it's much more relevant and entertaining to explain it in modern terms. We start with a press conference by, let's say the United Nations, who have discovered that the world is indeed enclosed in a giant, high tech dome of unknown origin and age.

The public reacts with wonder and awe, trying to take in the sheer scope of this announcement. Face book crashes, Twitter crashes, entire mobile networks crash. It's like hitting a bee hive with a sledgehammer. News organizations around the world send teams to the outer edge to confirm the finding, and the general public is glued to their media devices.

That's the good news, the excitement, the revelation, the positive shock. Then the bad news starts coming in waves, some of which you might not expect. The first is the immediate disbanding of NASA and all other world space programs, for obvious reasons. Most governments will secretly pardon these groups and keep them immune from class actions lawsuits, the lawsuits themselves coming from NASA investment groups, claiming fraud. Regardless, everyone at NASA despite their good intentions is out of a job overnight.

And this is where you would say good! They deserve it, about time they stopped lying to everyone. Oh but it doesn't stop there, because every contractor and subcontractor that are exclusively tied to NASA, they have to shut down as well. Fine, a few thousand jobs lost. No big deal.

And the ripples continue to spread, some bigger than others. Observatories all over the world close their doors, and the reasoning is this: If you've been looking at the ceiling for decades and couldn't tell it was a ceiling, then what good are you?

Every university in the world that has an astronomy or astrophysics program, well they don't anymore. Stephen Hawking? His book writing days are over. Carl Sagan? No more NOVA in syndication, I guarantee it. Those professors are going to have to retool their skills, and be prepared to answer one giant question. How did you now see it? Weren't their clues? People start finger pointing, and it will continue for years.

And still my fellow flat earthers will say, well hell, that doesn't sound too bad. So some nerds around the world lose their jobs, so what? You don't get off that easy, is what!

The finger pointing at the now defunct NASA will then turn to finger pointing at the government, who directed the whole thing. This is where we run into some dangerous ground, involving things like the Ark of the Covenant, the Holy Grail, and the ring of power.

And you say, ya lost me, I was with you until you started bringing up religious artifacts from movies. And you're supposed to be lost. Of the five major religions we mentioned earlier, those being Buddhism, Hinduism, Judaism, Islam, and Christianity, none have been able to produce a supernatural object over the last 5000 years, and trust me, it would be beneficial to do so.

The Ark of the Covenant would benefit Judaism, the Holy Grail Christianity, and the ring of power, well that benefits someone else, and maybe I'll leave alone for now. The point is that all religions are actively seeking their leverage against science. You've heard of the division between church and state, well here it is, advantage church. The barrier becomes a giant religious symbol, and since it is backed by the big five, it also becomes universal.

The big five then go into their drawer with the good silver and pull out this belief that was forgotten but not lost, and say, WE KNEW IT ALL ALONG, and science lied to us! Temporarily, all religions unite against science, which has been only moderately weakened by the removal of their astronomy and astrophysics divisions.

But the public won't care, because they will listen to the group shouting the loudest, and no one yells louder than the church. They will scream with righteous fury that the dome was built by OUR God, YOUR God, and the people will turn to science and hear nothing but crickets. And that's where the world changes, because in times of great stress, the public will want words, and while religion has no shortage of them, science simply is incapable of taking leaps of faith.

I'll take a glass half full approach and say that anyone listening to this is probably an intelligent rational person, one who can make informed decisions outside of the conventional doctrine. But for every one of you, there are hundreds, if not thousands of mouth breathing troglodytes who will not walk, but run to their respective house of religion and say: You were right about this, what else can you teach me?

This is what fills the current authority with pause. The unknown response to that question. Will religion take the high road and work with what remains of science to discover the truth? It's possible I suppose.

It's also possible that religion will combine this technologically advanced society with a revitalized and aggressive doctrine that then transforms daily life into something that makes the book 1984 seem like a Saturday morning cartoon show. I'm hoping that mankind will prove me wrong, but so far, that isn't the case.

So do some of your own research, and ask questions.

Clue 6
Depth Perception

This clue looks into the inevitable design question below the surface, or more specifically, how thick the flat earth design would need to be. To start, let's quickly recap the design features so far.

A basic dome structure, made up of advanced high density material thousands of miles wide, and at least 100 miles in height. The ceiling of said structure being projected upon by an ultra high definition system, using super LED technology and a combination of 2D and 3D imaging to simulate all celestial bodies including sun, moon stars, and so on. This ceiling is then protected by a scaling decrease in temperature and oxygen levels to the point where human life isn't naturally sustainable above 4 miles.

The lower surface of the domed structure consists of an organic layout of continents, grouped at the center, insuring that no land bridge exists to the outer ring. This is then surrounded by hundreds of miles of salt water in order to limit sea travel. The salt oceans are then adjusted with a scaling decrease in temperature as the outer area is approached, to the point where salt water freezes, forming icebergs, further reducing sea travel.

The outer ring is then elevated to a height of 10,000 feet, reducing oxygen levels, and a buffer zone of 300 miles is created. This zone is devoid of all life forms that could be used as food, further discouraging land travel.

That all sounds pretty good, but we left out one thing. Depth. Keeping human beings away from the ceiling is easy, because it requires higher technology. Protecting the outer ring is a little more difficult, but can be accomplished with layers of negative reinforcement.

Protecting the actual common ground is a different challenge, because digging is basic. Everyone knows how to use a shovel, and most construction requires a generous amount of digging. In addition, natural resources such as coal, oil, minerals, are harvested through large scale digging operations.

So it's safe to say that any human population is going to be digging a lot of holes, because it's easy, and necessary to continue their way of life. That being said, how thick would you need to make the flat earth model so that people didn't accidentally dig their way through?

You could use the same method as the outside barrier, and create a series of undesirable layers, ending in a solid barrier, but the ever expanding increases in general population would create an unnecessary risk. If the bottom of the flat earth was composed of say an unbreakable material, this would peak the diggers curiosity, and if repeated all over the world, would raise suspicions of design. While a solid barrier works at the end of a frozen wasteland where no one is venturing, or allowed, it doesn't do much if it's found in a mining quarry, or someone's backyard.

For that you need something that hasn't been used up to this point, a scaling increase in temperature, all the way to an ignition flashpoint, and then beyond.

Now you will jump in and say, well of course, we all know that there is molten rock below the surface. We see it in volcanoes, and well, volcanoes!

Yes, yes you do. And we've all seen the cross section diagram of the globe earth which shows ever brighter bands of molten structure and so on, which is why I included the Wiki link below[10] that covers the official view of the earth structure.

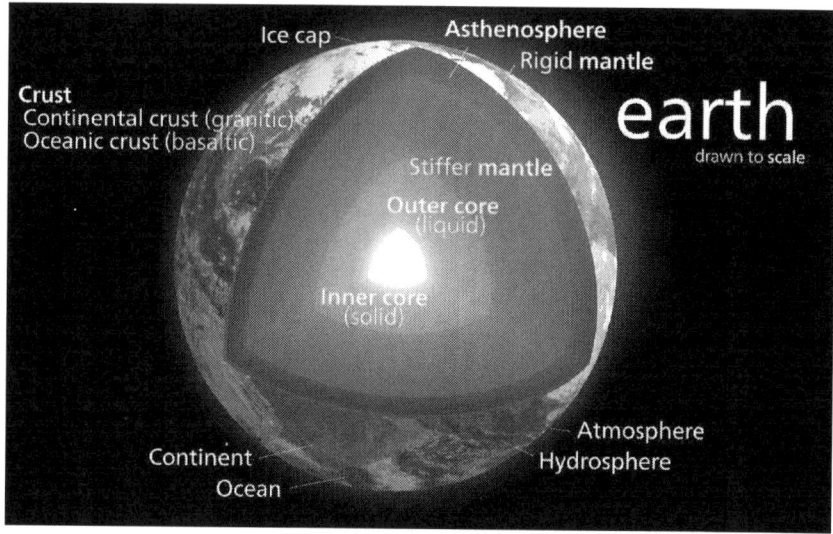

And I quote: "*Scientific understanding of the internal structure of the Earth is based on OBSERVATIONS of rock in outcrop, samples brought to the surface from greater depths by volcanoes, analysis of seismic waves, measurements of gravitational and magnetic fields and experiments with crystals at pressure and temperatures characteristic of the Earth's deep interior*".

In short? They have no clue on what's below them. None. In fact, the deepest holes ever drilled which I've also linked in the resources section only go down 8 miles. To repeat, **no one has gone below 8 miles, anywhere**. And every drilling

---

[10] https://en.wikipedia.org/wiki/Structure_of_the_Earth

survey is the same, a scaling increase in temperature to the point where drill bits stop working.

And you come back and say, but, Volcanoes! Yes there are volcanoes, holes in the earth where molten rock is produced, under pressure I might add. Certainly that can't be artificially created. No? We can melt rock right now; it's called a smelting plant. What do you think your car is made out of, melted, reformed, and polished rock.

We have the technology to do this, it all comes down to scale. Create a large set of furnaces at say, 50 miles below the surface that can melt and pump, molten rock. And you say, what would the furnaces be made out of? Oh I don't know, how about the same dome material than can withstand nuclear weapons?

So you take the molten rock, locate a few random access points on the surface, and the rest comes naturally. Volcanoes also reinforce the earth structure model that the molten rock goes all the way to the core, which then in turn reinforces the globe model and then we're back to where we are now. A smoldering globe flying through space at high speeds that from a design standpoint, makes no sense.

So how thick would the flat earth model floor need to be? Oh, for common use, say, less than 100 miles, similar to the ceiling in scale. Large heat generators placed in a pattern, a thin layer of molten rock 10-20 miles down, which is really just a geologic pipe system to help with the generation of terrain.

And there you have it, an efficient way of discouraging all those digging humans from reaching too far, combining a physical barrier with a mental one. 8 miles down and you're going to tell me what the entire core looks like?! Give me a break!

So do some of your own research, and ask questions.

Clue 7
The Long Haul

This clue looks into a topic I only glanced at in the original guide, which is the Southern hemisphere, or in the flat earth model, the land masses closest to the outer ring. I like to give credit where credit is due, and the long haul title was given to me by fellow flat earther who did some of the same research I did.

The summary of the video is this: If you are looking to show someone how to view the flat earth from a practical point of view, this is the example I would use. I'm going to show you how strange the world looks, using just a few web sites, some simple math, a couple minutes, and your brain.

You don't have to write anything down, unless you want to of course. I'll give you everything you need and break down one of the examples as well. I'll also link the sites used for reference.

FIRST!

Here are some websites that help you to calculate distance. The GPS on your phone already does this, and you may have an app as well, but here are some dedicated examples:

www.timeanddate.com
www.tripit.com
www.distancefromto.net
www.worldatlas.com
www.freemaptools.com
www.travelmath.com

If your favorite isn't listed here, (like Google maps), then use whatever is most familiar to you. Now we are going to look at two specific groups of cities. The first group is going be from the area around Australia, including New Zealand. We'll call it group one.

GROUP 1

Melbourne, Australia

Sydney Australia

Perth, Australia

Auckland, New Zealand

Christchurch, New Zealand

Hamilton, New Zealand

The second group is going to be some cities in South America, all in the Southern Hemisphere. I mention this because if you go high enough you will run into a few cities that won't work.

GROUP 2

Rio de Janeiro, Brazil

Sao Paulo, Brazil

Brasilia, Brazil

Buenos Aires, Argentina

Lima, Peru

Santiago, Chile

Again, there is a link[11] in the resources with many other airports. Now these two groups are interchangeable as you would imagine, so you can start or end with either group one or two, the results will be the same, and just to make it interesting, I'll use a slightly different example which a fellow

---

[11] https://planefinder.net/

flat earther did the legwork, and show you that even these two groups aren't exclusive.

So you take anything from group 1 and anything from group 2 and you get some distances, ranging from 6 to 8 thousand miles, roughly. That's all I want you to do here is get that part in your head, noticing that the route is bent, because they have to account for the curvature[12] of the earth. All these directions are what you expect, a straight shot over the South Pacific Ocean.

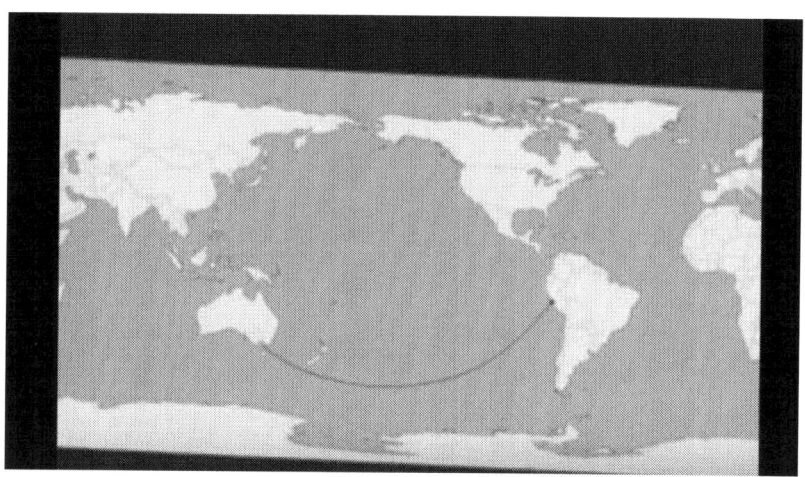

---

[12] Curvature of the earth is approx 8″ per mile. See this calculation in the FAQ – (question 3)

Now just to prove it's not an exclusive route, Instead of starting in say Rio and landing in Auckland, I'll start from what should be the opposite side in Cape Town South Africa, which is roughly the same distance on a globe earth, coming in at 7,300 miles.

Notice on the map it's still a straight shot through the Indian Ocean, and not crossing any countries. An easy route.

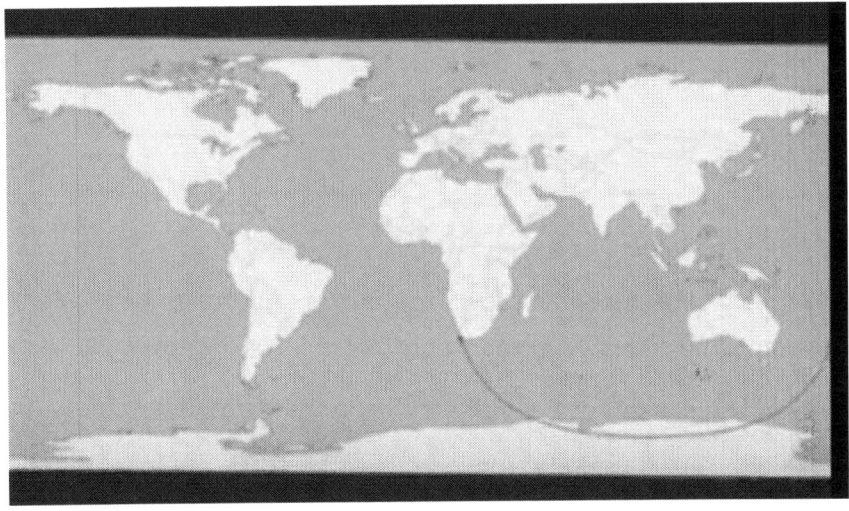

I try to book my flight. For this example we used travel math, but you can use whatever is easiest in your country, like *Price Line, Expedia, Travelocity*, it will make no difference because they're all tied into the same system. And this is when everything goes wrong.

So the first leg the airlines don't send me due East, but instead shoot me 4,700 miles almost due North, to Dubai. Ok, maybe we're just picking up people. Seems a bit excessive but I'll go with it. I'm probably comfortable in my seat drinking vodka tonics...

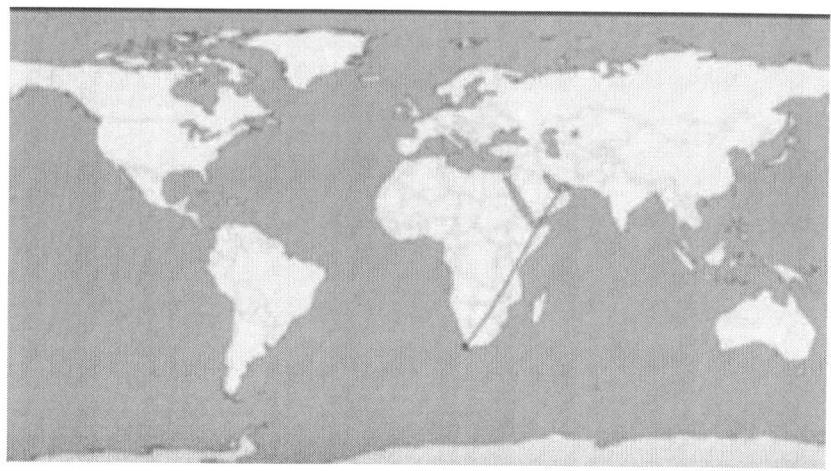

And from Dubai it should be a straight shot home to Auckland right? Err, no. Now they send me South East to Melbourne, a mere 7,300 miles. And then finally a third leg from Melbourne to Auckland coming in around 1600 miles. I'm rounding up or down to make the math easier. Regardless, the total miles for this flight is almost double what is expected, coming in at **13,600 miles**. In addition, the trip took me **37 hours**! How long should it have taken? In a 777, about 12.

Now this is where you come in and say, well, it's probably an isolated incident, or some strange connection thing. You know how the airlines are. Oh no my friends, we can do this all day. This roulette table is rigged, and there is no way to get a fair game!

The first part of the clue is the utter lack of non stop flights from anywhere in this hemisphere, which is why I gave you multiple cities in each group. And here's the plot hole for ya. Flying from international cities like Sydney, Rio, Santiago, or anywhere close by, you can't get a single non stop flight, no matter how much money you pay?

I tried to do this for an entire night, and it was like playing an online casino game, one that I was losing most of the time. The connections kept coming in like spam windows. Start in Christchurch, go to Auckland. Start in Auckland, go to Sydney. Start in Sydney, go to Dubai, or Los Angles, or somewhere else that makes no sense. Some of these connections took the trip over 50 hours to complete.

Go ahead, try it yourself. You may find one non stop, but even then the strangeness doesn't end there, because the speed is wrong. For reference I included an optimum cruising speed guide from a commercial pilot's forum that lists all the international aircraft used in these routes.

A 777, the current state of the art flagship plane, designed for maximum fuel efficiency, has a cruising speed of 640 miles an hour. 7,400 miles comes in at around 12 hours. Try to find this route. It doesn't exist. It can't. The closest I came was a 1 connection flight with a 3 hour layover. The total flight time was 20 hours. 20 take away 3 is 17, not 12. And this might work if the plane was doing, say 430 mph, but it's **not**. In fact, the slowest cruising speed I found was an older Airbus, just around 593. But this is all just numbers right?

It is until you pull up the flat earth map and look at the farthest two points, which just coincidentally are anywhere in Australia, and most of South America, or my example of lower Africa, which you can see isn't West at all...

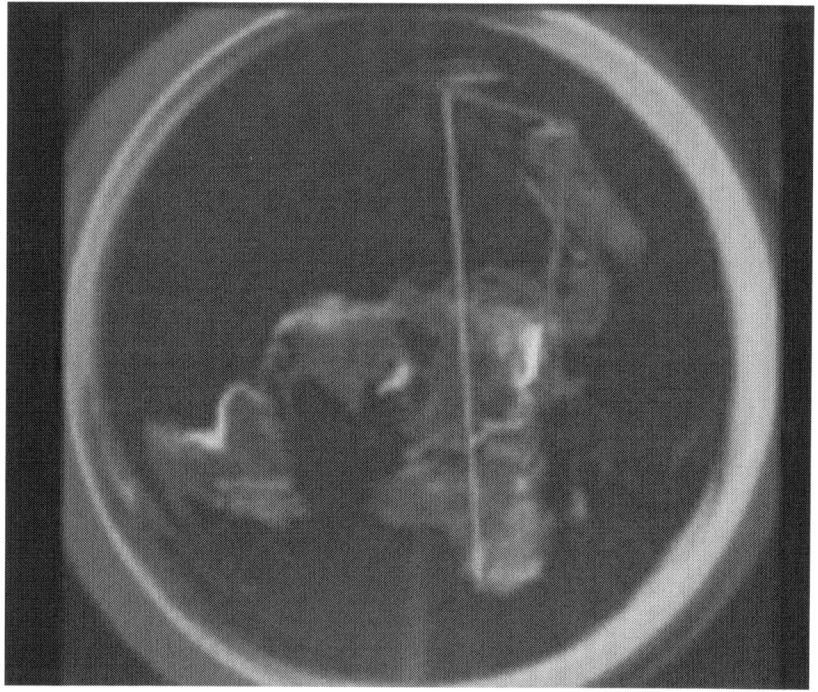

It's a shell game, and a very good one at that. Keep people guessing with multiple connections and layovers, jumping from city to city. People just sit in their seats, trying to sleep through it. And then it hits you, well the pilots would know right? They fly all day every day. Certainly they would have figured it out by now.

Some of them would get suspicious, sure. Any decent navigator would be able to work out the speed, fuel consumption, and odd connections, but imagine what they would have to get their head around?!

First, they would have to ignore the world GPS system that has been leading them to their destination without error. If you want some interesting side reading, check out the link on the history of the GPS[13]. And I quote, "*developed in 1973 to overcome the limitations of previous navigation systems, integrating ideas from several predecessors, including a number of classified engineering design studies from the 1960s*". Oh, and by the way, was created by the department of defense, the same people that closed off Antarctica.

GPS went fully live in 1995, so if you were a pilot before then, you might have been able to pick up a bread crumb trail. After that, very difficult. Plus, let's say you did figure that something was off, who exactly would you tell? The FAA? You would be looking around and wondering why you were the only one to see it, and then what?! You make the leap of faith and see that the entire map system is wrong? Never going to happen! You might as well just tell them that an alien spacecraft followed your plane around for 2 hours. We know what happens then...

Start playing flight time casino for yourself, see what interesting things you can discover, and while you're at it,

---

[13] https://en.wikipedia.org/wiki/Global_Positioning_System

show it to any pilots that you know, but don't forget to leave out the words "**flat earth**", because that's crazy, right?

So do some of your own research, and ask questions.

Clue 8
Creative Force

This flat earth perspective takes a look at the design from the ever present "**why ?**" standpoint; And although it will review some of the dome technical features already discussed, I'll try to do it from a different angle, or more specifically, why *I* might build it.

Someone mentioned to me recently that while the dome was a very big concept, it made the world much smaller, (kind of like what Admiral Byrd expressed in an interview all those years ago). This someone also said that it made them sad, which I understood, and while I did what I could to comfort this person, I realized that I could have done more, so this chapter is for the people who look upon this world with their new eyes and start drifting into a state of melancholy.

To preface, this isn't jail, nor are you lab rats, and before I'm done I hope to show you a version of *why*. To start, let's look at an old story, one that you may have heard, involving another enclosed world, kind of like yours. I say "*kind of like yours*" because the finished design that you are sitting in right now took several revisions in just about every aspect, much like any project. You come up with ideas, you see what works and what doesn't, and you improve the process until you come up with something that while not everyone agrees upon, satisfies the best of all criteria.

One of the first dome layouts involved a race of people who were supremely driven by ambition. They didn't have a word for lazy, or fear. They absorbed knowledge very quickly, incorporating physics, advanced electronics, engineering, and drove their technology with energy from the enclosed world itself.

And when their technology had reached the point where the dome structure was discovered in its entirety, there was no reaction of wonder and awe, they just looked up and squinted at the sky. Eventually, those squints turned into glares. Oh they had religion to be sure, and it was tied to their daily lives, but to them, this wasn't religion, it was a *challenge*, almost like they weren't that impressed.

Hard to fathom right? Seeing that your world had borders, but instead of being afraid, shaking your fist at the sky with arrogance? But that's what they did. So much confidence and might, that when they found out where they really were, a new priority was created.

At first they dedicated broadcast channels to calling the dome builders out, demanding answers, and ran them day and night. At the end of each cycle, the words kept repeating. **We know**.

But arrogance ebbs at patience, and their demands were met with silence, which was taken as blatant dismissal. This fueled their ambition even more.

The people withdrew all their efforts from breaching the outer barrier and formed a new plan. If the creators were not going to submit, then they would build a bridge and meet them at the gates!

So a building was designed, but to call it a "*building*" was to call the pyramids a sand castle. It was the greatest structure ever conceived, at least to them. It was to be over 30 miles wide, and hundreds of miles high, enough to reach the dome ceiling itself, where they would meet the builders face to face. They abandoned nature completely, and pushed aside ecologic systems to accomplish their goal.

They cannibalized entire mountain ranges, which they used to admire and love, to acquire the raw material for the awesome structure.

The work crews built with flawless precision, and it was obvious that it was going to succeed. A bridge to the edge of the sky itself. The work would only pause long enough for the mighty armies below to look up and yell "WE COME FOR YOU!" so loudly that on a clear day you could actually feel the dome shake.

And the creators, faced with their first great challenge, decided to start again. And the people were changed, their language fragmented so that the builders couldn't continue. The tower was dismantled, their technology removed and forgotten, and the people scattered.

A new group was introduced to the dome, divided in every way imaginable, so that unity was next to impossible, and everything slowed down. Languages evolved and devolved into other dialects, and the languages produced text which produced different forms of culture, and some amazing things began to happen, the most important of which was the arts.

The dome builders saw the artistic pool develop into several distinct forms. Everything drawn, in any medium on a flat surface, everything molded that took on a three dimensional shape, everything that produced music, all things that make up the human form in motion, and all the written works.

Pictures, sculptures, music, dance, literature. THE ARTS. Driven by passion, it is the very essence of what is good in humanity. Once this was recognized, all dome methods put in place were to cultivate and enhance this process. Land masses were adjusted with geology and temperature to support every kind of terrain with mountains, rivers, oceans, plains, forests, jungles, deserts, all of it stunning, all of it stimulating the human mind, nourishing it.

And the modifications continued, with seemingly endless shades of weather. The sky was overhauled, a moon added, and layers upon layers upon layers of stars, so that one day, when the people were able to see further than their eyes, there would still be something to new to see.

And the arts flourished, but there was a cost. The languages and division of cultures had put the population at odds, and wars were raging at regular intervals. The dome builders debated if the price was too high. Plans were drawn up to make more changes, until they noticed that the arts thrived even though the worst of conflicts, producing grace and beauty despite their burning world.

It was wonderful and terrible at the same time, and the debate outside the barrier continued to intensify until a majority spoke out and said, this world is a CREATIVE FORCE, and we must see what it leads to. The barrier must be hidden at all costs.

So the globe model was put into the population, and both science and religion adapted to it. The ARTS grabbed onto it like a new drug, the creative minds of the world exploding with new concepts. Their universe was now infinite, and the rules changed. Science then led to science fiction, which opened up everything else.

Books, pictures, sculptures, dance, and music, all reaching deep into space. Decade after decade of wonderful possibilities, rising above the ashes that were at their feet.

And it's not just the artists, it's everyone. You affect others who affect others, who inspire others, who build it, paint it, sculpt it, sing it, who then put it up on a pedestal and hold it under the light and say, THIS IS A PIECE OF WHO WE ARE. And for every one of them there are hundreds of others who for whatever reason were unable to express the songs and images and stories that are in their heads.

Imagination is far more important than knowledge, because it is limitless. It is your shield, your sword against the cruelty of destructive forces. There are those right now who live in chaos, who's life is surrounded by a swirling nightmare from which they think they'll never escape. These are the true warriors of the world, and they are far braver than me. I am humbled by those who suffer the most. Know that mountains were built for you, oceans were built for you. ALL OF THIS was built for you, your struggles, and your trials by fire.

It may be today, it may be tomorrow, but one day, the curtain will close and this stage will be struck, and when the dust settles, no matter where you are right now, you'll see the big picture, and have new eyes, and you will be shown, what wonder really is.

And as you leave this most magnificent of theatres, heading towards the next, my hope is that you'll pause, look back at the stage and say, I was actually in it you know, right there in the thick of things, and it was a sight to see. Because it really is a hell of a ride. Imagine what the next one will be like.

Clue 9
Magic Show

This flat earth perspective initially started out as a problem solving exercise that was going to just be built into clue 7, otherwise known as **The Long Haul**, but after some research, and a little patience, has evolved into something that warranted it's own section, and a perfect example of "good things come to those who wait"….

So emails and phone calls have been coming in, (almost all of them positive). Several people from around the world commented on the Southern plane routes. They said that while 95% of the long routes in that hemisphere were connections, (which in itself raises red flags); there were a few pesky non stops that seemed to contradict the overall logic.

The question then posed to me was obviously, **"Are they real flights?"** Could they be put there to throw the flat earth group off? If it was a trick, could I figure out what it was, and how it was accomplished? I accepted the challenge, and started my impression of Morgan Freeman as he went up against the four horseman magician crew.

Now admittedly, I was skeptical to start, because the flights went against the third rule - that being **the flat earth has no shortcuts**. Only a globe has shortcuts. As in magic, I had to assume the rule was not being broken, but only "hidden", or having the *illusion* of being broken.

But first, I had to see the trick itself. I had to see the planes in question, and see them make the route. Anyone can list a flight, but does it **actually** go from point A to B? With the help of several other people, this was then put to the test....

While just about everyone with a cell phone knows about GPS and how it can track things, many people don't know that even though it's a system built by the military, there is a very public aspect to it. So while your phone is tracked at all times, so are other things, most notably, all air traffic.

Now if you're *military*, you can view *military planes*. If you work at a cargo carrier like UPS or FEDEX, you can view transport planes. The general public is mostly limited to *commercial air traffic*. This can be viewed in several places, and the one I chose was *PlaneFinder.net*.

You can use others like *Flight Aware, Flight Radar, Flight Tracker*, it makes no difference, because they all are tied into the exact same GPS system. All these sites do basically the same thing. **Track every commercial plane in the world, from start to end, in real time**.

So I spend day after day looking at the plane finder global map, which you see below. At any given time, it's tracking between 3 to 7 thousand flights that are en route, anywhere in the world. You'll notice two different colors for planes, red and yellow. Yellow just means there is a 5 minute delay in processing, and only applies to the US.

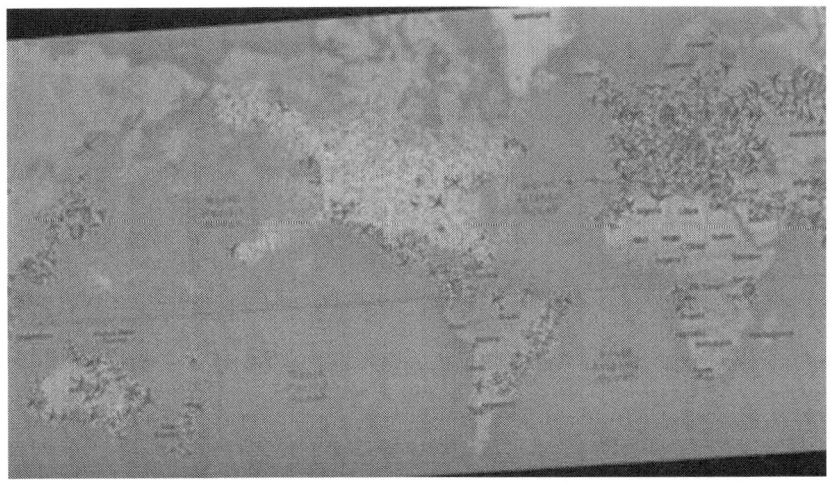

The point here is in order to prove out these flights that go against flat earth theory; I need to watch a few as they cross either the South Pacific, or Indian oceans. The web page updates automatically, but just to be sure, I close and reopen the page every 30 minutes or so, and wait for an ocean plane.

And I wait, and I wait, and I wait some more. Hours pass, days pass, and no red planes to entertain me. And somewhere in this process of me just staring at these empty oceans, waiting for a plane to cross, something occurs to me. Can you guess what it is? Nothing is crossing these oceans. Not non stops, connections, multiple connections, **nothing**.

But that's not possible right? The planes have to reach their destination! So I change gears and just watch the coastlines of anything in the Southern hemisphere, and I start to see it…. I follow a simple plane out of Brazil, on its way to South Africa, (which by the way is not part of the long haul argument). It's offshore just a few hundred miles. I get something to drink, and when I come back, it's gone! Hmmm.

Just a glitch right? So I follow another, and another and the same thing happens again and again. Once the plane reaches an imaginary line in the water, GPS makes it disappear. Then a friend who is also working on this problem sends me some links, which I've included in the resources[14].

---

[14]

http://uk.flightaware.com/live/flight/QFA27/history/20150228/0150Z/YSSY/SCEL/tracklog

I encourage you to look at them.

At first they don't seem like much, just an average flight log showing speed, altitude, location, things you could expect. Then you scroll down to about 3:30 in the morning, and the location drops away, and is replaced by either the word "*approximate*" or "*estimated*". This then continues for the next five hours, until miraculously, one hour before landing the flight log reestablishes itself, and the GPS system shows the plane in real time about to reach its destination!

So to be clear to those who may not be seeing everything here. The flights are being dropped off GPS, and their flight data is turned off, and stays off, until they are almost on top of their arrival point. And you say, well, that's how GPS works. Well no, because the Northern hemisphere has planes flying all over their oceans!

And then you say that *maybe it's a localized Southern hemisphere thing*. And I say, then why are all the flights over or near land perfectly tracked? Furthermore, this is a US based system, with Americans flying on vacation every single day. You're telling me that those people aren't going to be tracked?

In addition, the vanishing plane act is happening to not only the South Pacific and Indian Oceans, (which I would expect), but also the South Atlantic, which isn't part of the flat earth argument. There are a bunch of flights that cross this relatively small ocean between South America and Africa, and every one of the planes is hidden shortly after takeoff.

So then you say, what would be the purpose of hiding those shorter routes in the Atlantic? It's because of something I didn't see right away. If you hide one flight, you have to hide them all. Showing the GPS routes in the Atlantic but leaving out the Pacific and Indian oceans would raise different questions, so the logic here, (despite being very sneaky), is sound.

The third rule is that the flat earth has no shortcuts. If you look at the Azimuthal Equidistant map again, and look close, you notice that while the South Pacific, South Atlantic, and Indian oceans make up the lower section on a globe, they make up the outer ring on a flat model.

In that model, there is no shortcut between Australia and South America. If you are creating flight routes, you have only two choices. You take the long way around, clockwise or counterclockwise, and stay on the ocean, or you cut across the land in the middle. But if you cut across land, you have to create connections, because on a globe it wouldn't make sense to fly over the top of the United States to get to South America.

Neither of these choices is ideal, so the authority came up with a compromise. Disable GPS and lose the planes for every ocean flight in the Southern hemisphere, then reactivate them once the destination is reached. This is just one of the lengths that they are willing to use to keep you from seeing it. Don't just hide some things; hide *everything*, so that maybe, the topic isn't addressed.

And some would come back and say, *well nice going, you've just pointed out a flaw in their system, and sooner or later, they will fix the gap*. Hmm, maybe. But not soon I think. Remember this is a rule, not a guideline. They can't change the map, so they have to work within its limitations. If they have a better workaround I can't wait to see it.

So do your own research and ask questions, Oh, by the way, welcome to the flat earth, and enjoy your flight.

Clue 10
Hiding God

As you can tell from the title, I'm taking a different approach. Eventually, I was going to have the address the question of *What happens next?* Or *what do we do now with the information at hand?*

If you've made it through the guide, and the first nine clues, then at this point you're either buying into the flat model, or on the fence. If this is the first clue you went to because of the title, I recommend you go back, because we're not going to do much in the way of reviewing.

But if you're still with me, then you would agree that:

1. The world you've been taught has been kept from you, and

2. One way or another, you would like to prove this out.

So how is this possible? The authority in question who created what you call "the globe" is guarding all the gates. They protect the sky, the outer edge, and most importantly, the education system that shows us at an early age what they WANT us to see.

Nobody reading this has their own spaceship, or advanced rocket program. Nobody actually owns a long distance ice breaker. And while some of you may have a private plane, I wouldn't recommend testing a military barrier that technically, doesn't exist.

But then again, you have to remember that this is not the story of David and Goliath. The hidden world was never going to be sustainable forever. As a civilization evolves, the tools the authority uses as a method of control become more vulnerable. I've learned many things about systems over the years, and one thing that I find most interesting is that as layers of strength increase, the higher the chance that they can be used to your advantage.

But maybe I'm talking in riddles. I should be boiling it down to what **can** be done, by showing you what's being hidden, what's *important*, and how it can be spread to others without looking like a crazy person.

To be clear, and I can't stress this enough, **DO NOT start conversations with the word FLAT EARTH**. Think of it like Fight Club. The first rule of Flat Club is that you **DO NOT** talk about Flat Club. Before you started waking up and reading all these things you were like me, you laughed and mocked everything that was flat earth. You may have learned faster than others, but the knee jerk reaction by 99% of the people was created the day they sat down in a classroom and stared at the globe.

Look at the videos. Not just mine, but others who are putting forward some great arguments, and ask the questions that people can relate to. I'm going to introduce three very important questions that you can use. Each with a statement that precedes it, and each statement is a motivation for a different group of people. If you don't fall into one of these three groups, then I guarantee you know people that do.

The first statement is this: **YOU ARE BEING HIDDEN.**

What do I mean by that? Well this goes back to Clue 7 and Clue 9, which talk about the flights in the Southern hemisphere. If you are flying on a plane over the Southern hemisphere, you're flight is **NOT** being tracked.

How can this be used to find out the truth? It's simple, it's quick, and it costs no money. No matter what country you live in, send a quick note to your local, state, or federal representative, and ask them this question: **Why are citizens of our country flying over oceans without the SAFETY NET of the GPS system?** And remind them that GPS stands for GLOBAL, not partial. Without GPS anything could happen to your plane, and no one knows where you are!

And while you're at it, remind them that the GPS system was built by the United States department of defense, who NEVER does anything small. The system that is in effect now has what appears to be HUGE deliberate gaps in the Southern hemisphere only. **Do not mention FLAT EARTH!** Just voice your concern about the SAFETY of you, your loved ones, and your fellow citizens.

Will they get back to you? Possibly. Will they give you a satisfactory answer? Not a chance, because they will only have what the military gives them. What this will do however is create a unique buzz in certain circles that may prove to be useful later. The more politicians or high ranking officials you contact, the greater the noise. The motivation here, (as you can tell), is **general public concern.**

The second statement is this: **WEALTH IS BEING HIDDEN.**

What do I mean by that, goes back to Clue 2 and every other mention regarding Antarctica. In 1954 it was announced on *national television* that the continent was just millions of miles of rich energy resources, and by 1959 it was sealed off like Area 51.

How can this be used to find out the truth? By contacting anyone you know in either the petroleum, natural gas, or mineral industry. This means *Exxon Mobil, British Petroleum, Royal Dutch Shell, Chevron, Conoco Phillips, BHP Billiton, Rio Tinto, Glencore, Anglo American*, and there are many others.

Find anyone in these companies and make inquires about their prospects in Antarctica. Send them the link to the Admiral Byrd interview [https://www.youtube.com/watch?v=czW0iRJuH1A], and ask them why if there are no environmental conflicts regarding oil, gas, or mining, why aren't they allowed to even petition the idea, even when the world's energy resources are dwindling more every day.

Put the sound of money in their ear. They may not be able to break through the decades of red tape laid out in front of them, but it will create a buzz from a different side: the motivation of greed, and of pristine resources just begging to be harvested.

And finally, to preface the third statement, I need to thank all the people who have sent me stacks and stacks of biblical scripture, asking me to stop dancing around the title of the flat model, and call the structure what it really is.

And you know, they have a point. I have put myself at a distance, because I wanted to reach people who were outside of religious faith, and even outside of general conspiracies. But for all those spiritual groups that have contacted me, I can now however, say with conviction that:

The third statement is this: **THEY ARE HIDING GOD**

Despite what labels I put on the flat model structure, the oldest names are from the oldest texts, one of those being called the firmament. If the firmament was indeed discovered in 1956, and it was ***deliberately hidden***, then the ruling authority not only hid the structure, but evidence of the builders, and by "builders" I mean "creators", and by that I mean what people define as GOD.

Hiding GOD could be considered one of the worst ideas of all time, and if you are a person of great or small faith, you have a vested interest in any evidence that would solidify and vindicate your years of dedicated service. If a structure was found that had, for all intents and purposes the handprint of GOD on it, then the ruling authority has no right to keep it from you!

There are billions of people on this world who have personally dealt with the concept of GOD, and would like to know for sure, if these beliefs are well placed, or, in short - you want to know the meaning of life? It's out there, and it's been hidden from you. Your motivation is clear. Go to your church leaders, your congregation, and tell them science probably found evidence of GOD in 1956, and decided to keep it a secret.

If you know people of religious power, send this up the ladder, get the word out, and see what comes back.
Between these three statements and questions people will talk to people, who will talk with others, and eventually, reach someone WHO **KNOWS**.

This isn't a *grassroots* or *groundswell* movement that takes a long time. Because the system that has been used to mold and control you these past years has been based on SPEED, and by that I mean **REAL TIME**. All it takes is a single video, a memorandum, one whistleblower, one key person, and everything changes, not in months or weeks or days, but **HOURS**.

And in those hours, everything changes, because of the speed. People all over the world wake up, and look at the sky with new eyes, and things start to get better.

One person - that's all it takes! One person to come forward, and share what has been hidden for so long. Maybe someone who is tired of all the games, maybe someone who has gone year after year burdened by such a heavy secret. Maybe you, who are reading right now, who was looking for a reason to come forward. This is it.

And if you don't want to walk into the light and be the hero, I understand. But if you can't, for whatever reason, then be anonymous, share the message, and help us make this world better, because it CAN be better.

For everyone else, give this person an opening, give them the opportunity, and give them the support they need to help reclaim what's left of our civilization, because we need it now more than ever.

I will keep spreading the word for as long as I can, in hopes that everyone that hears it starts seeing things with new eyes, and I encourage each of you to do the same, and maybe one day, we will learn to treat others better than we treat ourselves.

Clue 11
Souls In The System

This clue looks into the recent past, or more specifically, an odd but interesting piece of conspiracy lore. What I hope to show here is an example of how an enclosed system, once revealed can change the world very quickly, and in ways you may not have realized.

To start, we need to go back a little ways, to a controversial 2004 documentary called *"Astronauts Gone Wild*[15]*"*. For those of you who missed this strange little gem, the summary is this: The producer/director Bart Winfield Sibrel, went out to prove that all the moon landings were elaborate hoaxes. To do

---

[15] https://en.wikipedia.org/wiki/Astronauts_Gone_Wild

this, he set up interviews with the Apollo astronauts, giving them the impression that the interview was just routine.

He then produced a bible, and asked each of the astronauts to swear on the book before the interview started. The interview was then supposed to be a series of detailed technical questions designed to trip up the astronauts. During the process, there was quite a bit of tension and some very uncomfortable moments, including one actual fist fight!

Now I'm not recommending that anyone actually go out and watch this hour long documentary. For me, the astronauts have had to live with this guilt a long time, and leaving them alone seems like the humane thing to do.

What interested me, and moreover, what peaked my interest **then**, wasn't the unoriginal questions the reporter posed, but how the astronauts reacted to the bible itself. None of the Apollo pilots would put their hand on it and swear that they went to the moon! In fact, most treated the book like it was made of plutonium. This puzzled me for years, because it went against the basic rules of any cover up, one of which is, **lie about everything**.

Now, the pilots of the Apollo program had done many interviews over the years, many televised, and had been going through their song and dance without really any instances of contention. So why not just go through the motions again. It is after all, just a book, right?

People lie under oath all the time - its called perjury. And every country has an extensive system of laws and punishments to deal with it. These punishments don't seem to stop the people from committing perjury, and you can read about it almost every day. Furthermore, the astronauts were not IN court. This was just a room, (sometimes their own home), so swearing on the book would for all intents and purposes, be meaningless.

And this sat in the back of my head for years, because it didn't make sense. Why would astronauts, trained by a very large science program, be afraid of just putting their hand on the book and just tell one more lie? Well for them, it may have been more than *just a book* - it may have been a symbol of something much bigger...

You see, for you, me, and almost everyone else, a holy book is a symbol of **faith**, because the creator or creators have yet to be revealed. But if you **KNEW** that the creators were real, then the book becomes something much more tangible, more relevant, and more sobering.

Or more to the point, the Apollo astronauts would have been let in on the enclosed system during their tenure with NASA and over the decades, this system created certain truths for these men, one of which is, someone could be watching. Now, whether the builders/creators are actually watching every little thing we do can be debated, but if you have proof that they are real, then the thought of your every move being scrutinized is a very real possibility.

This is what you and I may **suspect**, but don't **feel**. The Apollo pilots however, are a different story. If they were **shown** how the world really looked, then their attitude towards the book takes on a whole new meaning. In fact, it didn't have to even be a bible. It could have been an encyclopedia, or a piece of wood, because it was the **IDEA** that made them pause.

And if you're still not getting it, then I'll ask you directly. *If you actually saw some of the creators handiwork, and knew that there was a chance you were being watched, and there was a scorecard involved, would you swear against that and lie about something? Would you roll those dice and take the chance?* Or to put it another way, everyone has gotten frustrated about something, then looked up and cursed the sky. *Would you still do that if you knew that a creator was up there and possibly listening?*

That's how knowledge of the enclosed system changes people. The astronauts didn't want to roll the dice and lie, because there was a real fear of retribution; and while they were confident that a bolt of lightning wasn't going to strike them down, they also weren't going to push their luck.

And we all take on the same approach in daily life. Everyone who drives has run a stop light. We know when we see the yellow light that it's too far away, so we hit the gas and hope for the best , (especially if the traffic is light and we aren't putting anyone in danger).

But you take that very same intersection, and put a red light camera on it, well, then things change don't they? Do you hit the gas and roll the dice? Not a chance. You hit the brakes and hope that you can stop in time, because you are being watched. You may not be a model driver by any sense of the word, but you understand this rule and this place, and you don't break it.

And this one aspect is why I'm pushing so hard to see the enclosed system revealed, because as a civilization, we seem to be only as good as what we can get away with. This isn't an issue with freedom; it's an issue with doing the right thing. You know that running red lights is a bad idea. The camera is a reminder of that. Imagine all the things that would change for the better if the enclosed system was revealed. Would you lie to hurt someone? Would you rob a bank, commit fraud, or embezzle? Would you steal anything, unless your life depended on it?

And while people would still get angry and fight, would they maim each other? Would they kill? Would anyone knowingly commit murder? Would you bully or extort people for profit? In fact, knowing that your world was created, would you do ANYTHING malicious towards anyone?

103

If the world is not a globe, but instead enclosed then wars end, hate crimes end, (maybe not overnight), but quickly, because you may be, for the first time in your life, actually accountable for your actions. You realize now that you are a very real soul in this enclosed system, and you have a responsibility towards your fellow man, one that can be boiled down into one simple rule: **Treat others better than you treat yourself.**

This, THIS is why it's so important to show the world as it really is. This is why I am asking the AUTHORITY itself to OPEN THE DOOR, and let this secret come through. You've kept this HIDDEN for too long, and the people who live here with you have been through enough.

This isn't about money or power anymore - it's about our very souls, the essence of who we really are. Wealth and titles don't define your heart. Hiding the entire world may have seemed like a good idea at the time, but we have gone way beyond that. Have you actually seen our home recently? This needs to be fixed, and it needs to be now. The people won't forget the deception, but they will forgive you for it, because a truth like this will make them nobler, something we should have been since the beginning.

So do your own research, and always, ALWAYS ask questions, because that's the only way you will find all forms of the truth.

Clue 12
Real Eyes

This clue covers an enclosed system feature which for me at first seemed like just a necessary aspect of the process - that being what we perceive with our own eyes, because for many, that's the validation we need. Can seeing things with our eyes really be trusted though? The more I looked into it, the more it became apparent that they cannot.

In fact, it became obvious that as a species, we seem to have layers of cognitive weakness, especially when it comes to optical perception, like it was built into our very genetic code.

Layers that naturally help things like hiding the shape of the world. I'm going to show you some examples, and before this clue ends, you'll know why everyone else around you is missing the big picture, and just how rare you are to realize it.

For example, what is this object? It's your world.

Image of the Day Earth from Space: from earthobservatory.nasa.gov

This is where you live. You know it as certain as anything else that's given, like gravity, temperature, and touch. But you can't touch or see your world, like this, so if I take this image away, how do you still know?

Anyone who has followed the clues so far know that I for the most part just use some slides and a narrative, but some of the best optical examples use moving illusions, so for better or worse, I'll be including small sections of video into this clue to help drive home the point. [It would be a good idea to watch this video clue online][16].

So let's start with a dramatic entrance, something you can relate to. This is for all the questions regarding the sky, and how things can be accomplished. To this, I have to remind people using a Truman show example, where the director, living in the moon structure, queues the sun. Keep in mind this is a very small enclosed system. If the sun, moon, and stars can be reproduced here, imagine what you could do with a dome 1000 times larger using technology far beyond ours.

But maybe I'm getting ahead of myself. Like the mice in clue 4, we should start with something small, because the small stuff is easy to figure out, right? Take this spinning ballerina, for example. If I say that she's spinning on her left foot before you look, then she spins on her left foot. If you look away and I now say she's spinning on her right, then when you look again she's now on her right, but try to change her direction while staring directly at her, and it becomes much more difficult.

[16] https://www.youtube.com/watch?v=ditQ1BfwlRA – Clue 12 (video)

Did I change her graphic? Is it magic or witchcraft? Not at all. How the girl is animated gives your mind the choice of how she is spinning, you just need a starting point. So you say, well, that's an animation, just a clever trick. So I show you this still picture of a match and its shadow against the wall. Notice anything missing?

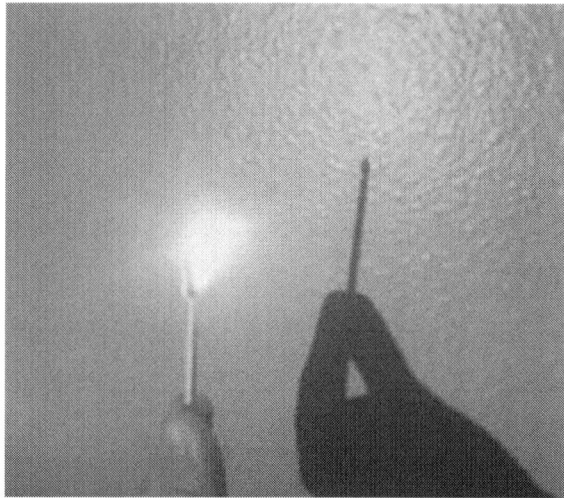

Like the shadow of the flame itself? Your mind wants it to be there, but it isn't. Everything casts a shadow, right? Your eyes want the image to include the flames shadow, even though logic tells you the pure light source can't have one.

And then there's the famous dress, which is in real life is blue and black, but how it's photographed gives the human mind an option of seeing it in gold and white. You know what color it is, because you can see it, but if someone else sees a completely different color, then who's correct? If everyone in the room sees black and you see gold, are you wrong because you're in the minority? And what does that say about possible illusions that can be tailored to a small group of people, or just you?

Human eyes are easy to manipulate. Take this classic example. If you stare at the four dots in the center for 30 seconds, then turn away and look at something white, then you will see a residual image of a bearded man, but that's not the trick.

It's that the residual image is in color, even though you were staring at something black and white, showing you that your eyes can be conditioned in a relatively short amount of time.

And speaking of black and white, let's see if you can avoid a simple distraction. Watch the video: https://www.youtube.com/watch?v=ditQ1BfwlRA from 5 minutes 21 seconds in. Focus on white, and try to see how many passes are made by the white colored team. Can you tune out everything else and count the number of white passes? You're confident that the total number of passes is 13, and congratulations, you would be correct, but this wasn't about the number of passes, it was about the bigger distraction.

By following the white team you were ignoring the black team, and moreover, everything black, so you failed to see the dancing black bear that was right in front of you. Don't worry, I didn't see it either the first time, and, being that you now know how it's done, you can't be fooled again, right? Rewind and try it, still focusing on the number of passes, and see if you can catch the bear. It's harder than you might think.

[Still watching the same video as above] - Many people will see this dragon and think it's a computer generated effect.

It's actually very real, but the illusion only works from certain angles. If you walk too far one way or the other, you can see behind the scenes.

If you cannot see behind the scenes, your mind can't break out of the illusion, no matter how hard you try.

And this then leads us back to something that shouldn't be a trick, but is. It's called the Mercator map[17] [below].

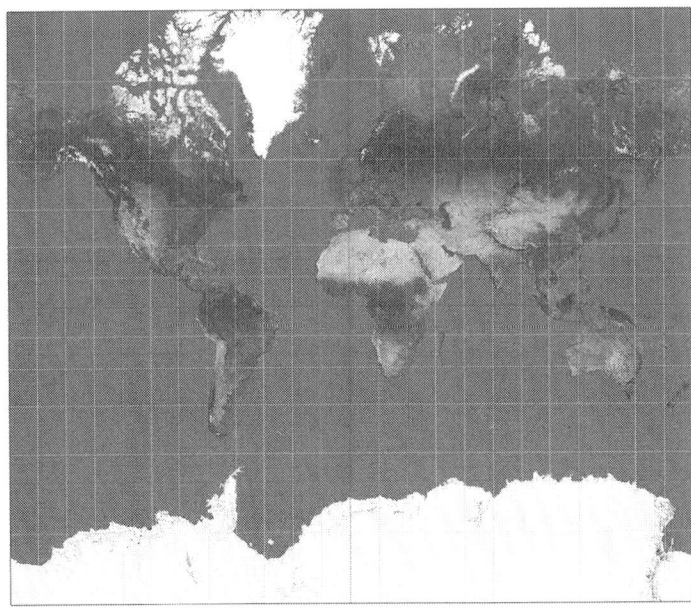

[17] https://en.wikipedia.org/wiki/List_of_map_projections

And you say that it's not a deception, it's a real map. How do you know this? Because it was on a wall in your school classroom? All geographers in the world know that this map is **very wrong**.

The correct perspective map is this, the Gall Peters [below].

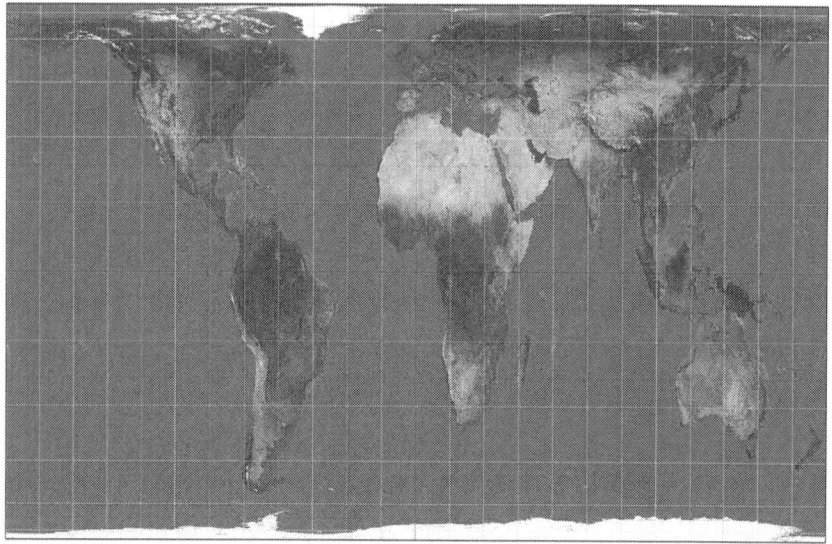

It shows countries how they actually are in comparison to each other. This is the map that should be in schools right now, but the authority thinks you'll be more comfortable with the old map.

You say that they aren't that much different, that at least the location is correct right? Take a look at the size of Europe, and where Germany is.

We assume, like many things that what is presented to us is the truth, because we want to believe, and I mean that literally. Human beings as a species are designed to believe what they see. It's called **suspension of disbelief**.

Think you're immune to this disbelief process? Why do you get emotional when watching a movie? You know it's a movie, you know that you're watching just a two dimensional image on a screen. You've seen the actors before many times in other films, and you know that the process to make the film took hundreds of people and millions of dollars to create. But if the story is convincing enough, you will forget all that, at least for a while, and be swept up in the moment.

But enough tricks, what about real life? Without all the slight of hand and distraction, you should be able to determine everything as it really is, right? Don't be so sure. Ever driven a car in stop and go traffic, zoned out for a bit, then had that horrifying feeling that you couldn't tell if your car was moving, or the car next to you was moving? That happens to all humans.

University studies on motion perception have been done for years and they determined if the movement was smooth enough, human beings couldn't tell the difference between our motion, and the motion of other objects. This applies to cars, trains, basically any vehicle you may be in, maybe even one as large as the world itself.

113

To be clear, you can't really tell if your car or train is moving. No one can. It's an assumption. So now tell me that you can feel your world spinning at 1000 miles an hour, and rushing around the sun at 60 times that speed.

Your world isn't spinning, or moving forward - only the sky is - and even that isn't real. The stars spin, the moon circles, as does the sun. All of it built with great craft and precision, to create the illusion that you are isolated in a vast universe, to fend for yourself, which is not the case.

Or, in short, we were designed to believe, to accept the illusions as reality, so that an enclosed system could be built around us, and we could live in it without the burden of confinement.

And for those of you who still haven't used their real eyes yet, here's one more trick. See if you can solve it.

Real eyes. Realize. Real lies.

Final Words

At the time of this writing, the Flat Earth Clues video series is exactly one year old. I had woken up at 3:30 in the morning on February 10, 2015 with the narrative in my head. It's hard to believe how much has happened since then. A movement has grown, science is bracing on all fronts, and more than anything else, people have started doing their own research, and are still asking questions. Every day I found myself looking at this Flat Earth with a new perspective. One of the more interesting questions I get is: **Now that my eyes have been opened, how do I approach others?**

Before you tell them anything, remember how long it took you to understand where you now live. They will also need that kind of time. The shortened introduction I now tell people goes something like this:

Before you were born, before your parents, your grandparents, before you even had a family line - there was the illusion, the trick, the lie - that you lived on a small spinning rock, flying through space.

You thought it was true, because children don't believe in lies. And you grew up, and it was still true, because science is never wrong.

Except for small things like: Lead Gasoline, Lead Paint, DDT, Cigarettes not causing cancer, and what the core of the earth looks like.

You know that fire burns, water is wet, drop something and it falls to the floor. We can all test these things. What shape is the world? That's not something you know, it's something you're *TOLD*. To put it simply, you just have to take their word for it.

And there's the real crux of the problem; the weight of their word, it's really about trust. Most of us trust science to some degree. To be fair, it has produced some modern conveniences, like air conditioning, light bulbs, and smart phones.

But it also made things like atomic weapons, nerve gas, and napalm. Make no mistake - the greatest advances in science have been in different ways to kill each other.

What if, after centuries of preaching the globe as a religious icon, "the powers that be" found out that it was actually not a sphere, but instead something much different? Would they risk unraveling 500 years of science doctrine by informing the public? Could a government still retain its authority if there were actually proof of a higher power?

It's about proving the Flat Earth, but more importantly, it's about *disproving* the globe, and that shouldn't be possible, but there are several big questions which science has a difficult time with.

Why was there only one blue marble image used for 43 years? Where are the videos of the earth rotating from space? Astronauts can't turn around in space with the camera running? Not even by accident? Are the Van Allen radiation belts dangerous? Why does the Orion Trial by Fire video exist? Why was the space shuttle program cancelled? Why does the Mars mission keep getting postponed? Why are they closing down the ISS (International Space Station)?

Why is Psalm 19:1 on Werner Von Braun's headstone? Why is the moon generating a light that is sometimes 12 degrees colder than the moon shade? How is that possible if it's reflecting the suns rays? And if the moon is generating its own light source, then what was that dark grey thing we landed on?

We can beam back crystal clear photos of Pluto, but the Global Positioning System doesn't track planes in the Southern oceans?

And why does **this** topic, compared to ANY other, (conspiracy or not), make people excited, angry, or scared? Some of you are getting anxious just listening! Why? Because it's the greatest trick of all, and we all fell for it. You should be excited, because it's going to change the world. You should be angry, because you were fooled your entire life, and you should be a little scared, because this is uncharted territory.

This is the Flat Earth theory - that the world is easy to understand, more intimate, and very deliberate. It didn't just happen. It was built, and more importantly built for you. Open your eyes and smile. You have never been alone.

Mark Sargent - February 10, 2016

FAQs
Answers to some frequently asked questions

So, at this point, you may have some questions, right? Over the past 12 months, having done literally dozens of interviews on various radio stations and with media outlets internationally, there have been some questions that have frequently popped up. To help you and the skeptics to navigate through the flat earth world, here are the answers to some of the most commonly posed questions.

Note – if you have any burning questions that aren't covered here, tune into http://truthfrequencyradio.com currently at 7:00PM Pacific Coast Time, USA and listen in to Strange World radio and ask your question there! All Strange World shows are posted on YouTube channel: MarkKSargent.

1. *If you flip the flat earth over, what do you see?*
No one currently knows what is underneath the enclosed world model, but then again we don't currently know what is below the globe model either. Remember that the deepest hole ever drilled by our civilization is only 8

miles/12 kilometers, and yet, mainstream science shows up detailed diagrams going all the way down to the center of the earth at 4000 miles. I believe that below 8 miles is the real machinery that runs this wonderful system we live in. Everything from the underwater conveyor system, to magma machines are housed there. Maybe even survivors of previous civilizations.

2. On the flat earth model, how does the sun and moon work? They never go below the horizon; they just get larger and smaller as they move closer and further away. The sun and the moon are radically different in the enclosed world model. The sun isn't 93 million miles away, nor is the moon 237 thousand miles away. They are both roughly the same size, and rotate over the disc surface like pieces of a mobile hanging over a child's crib. The sun is also a directional light source, similar to a spotlight, and the moon is its own light source, like a night light. So even though we have been taught that the sun falls over the curvature of the earth, in reality, they are just moving away from us, like a giant searchlight attached to a helicopter. The moon is also very interesting with its light source. Multiple tests have been done in 2015 that show the moonlight generating a refrigerated radiation, which actually cools objects. At the time of this writing, moonlight has been shown to chill items almost 13 degrees F, compared to items in moon shade, which is the opposite of what we see in sunlight. Look these tests up on YouTube and see for yourself!

3. What is the curvature of the Earth (according to mainstream science)?

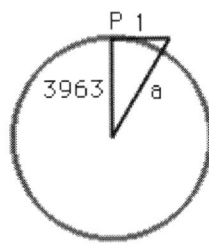

Suppose that the earth is a sphere of radius 3,963 miles[18]. If you are at a point P on the earth's surface and move tangent to the surface a distance of 1 mile then you can form a right angled triangle as in the diagram.

Using the theorem of Pythagoras:

$a^2 = 3,963^2 + 1^2 = 15,705,370$ and thus a = 3,963.000126 miles. Thus your position is 3963.000126 – 3,963 = 0.000126 miles above the surface of the earth.

0.000126 miles = 12*5,280*0.000126 = 7.98 inches. Hence the earth's surface curves approximately 8 inches in one mile. The curvature is 8 inches in the first mile, and increases with each mile squared. So at 2 miles is (2x2) x 8 inches, (3x3) x 8 inches and so on, until it reaches 3963 x 3963 x 8 inches, at which point it drops vertical into infinity, provided you believe the globe.

4. If the Earth is flat, why can't tall large objects be seen more than a few miles away? Why can't a person look at Mount Everest or the Empire State Building through a telescope? Why do tall objects gradually fall behind the horizon as you move farther away? Why does all vision end at the horizon,

[18] Models of Figure of the Earth -
https://en.wikipedia.org/wiki/Figure_of_the_Earth

regardless of weather conditions? Tall objects can be seen at great distances right now, especially over water, but there are limits to what the human eye can see through atmospheric conditions. Currently zoom lens technology has shown only recently that ships going over the water horizon aren't really gone at all, but just beyond the vanishing point of the eye. Once the boat disappears past the 8 inches per mile squared[19], it shouldn't come back with a better telescopic lens, but it does! There are many videos on Youtube regarding this.

5. If the Earth is flat, why is its shadow on the moon during an eclipse always round? All eclipses in the enclosed world model are artificial, like they would be in a planetarium, which is really what you are in, a giant planetarium combined with a terrarium. There is no Earth between the sun and the moon, so everything you see displayed in the sky, that being the sun, moon, stars and planets, are part of a fantastic display system. The only difference between this and what we build for educational purposes is that the sun and moon appear to be separate three dimensional objects with their own properties, which makes sense given how much time we spend looking at them. Remember that the moon is the most photographed object of all time.

6. If the Earth is flat, how do the sun and moon rise and set? This should be impossible. The sun and the

---

[19] 8″ per mile squared – calculation in question 3 of the FAQ

moon do not set in the enclosed world model, they just move further away from you, continuing their very long circle above the disc. A good representation of this would be the Ying/Yang symbol used in Asian cultures. Some in the movement believe that this symbol and how is shows light and darkness above a circle is no accident, but ancient knowledge.

7. If the Earth is flat, how do satellites orbit? If there are no satellites, how are satellite services provided in remote areas? (Don't say by ground antennas, such things don't exist in remote areas of the arctic or the middle of the ocean). Why do satellite antennas only work when pointed at one point in the sky? Who told you there were satellites to begin with, the same people who showed you pictures of the United States landing on the moon? I've personally combed the sky with night vision binoculars for years, and can tell you with confidence that the lights moving up there are NOT us. I'll go so far to say that the whole satellite concept is part of a cover to keep us from finding out that we aren't the first ones to rent this apartment, so to speak, and that remnants of older civilizations are using advanced technology and operate at altitudes far above commercial air traffic. For the satellite services, we have recent expert testimonials that state that all current satellite transmissions are using a modified version of the older LORAN system, and that anything pointed at the sky is just bouncing off the structure itself, then rerouted by

123

the powers that be. For more details please see "TESTIMONY SHOWS" on my Youtube channel.

8. If the Earth is flat, what keeps it from collapsing into a ball like all other large planetary bodies? Why are all other planets round? This question comes up every week, and people ask it because of their programming. If we are in a giant planetarium that creates the illusion of space, what makes you think there is ACTUAL space outside of this place? Outside of this structure there could be anything, a bigger room, more enclosed worlds, an unlimited dimension, or maybe just plain old water. Everything INSIDE the structure is to simulate space, the imagination, and the biggest reason of all: That we can't get off, and that there is no fence, and possible EXIT.

9. If there is no such thing as gravity, as some flat Earthers claim, what holds everything down? What holds the solar system and galaxy together? (Assuming flat Earthers even believe in these things)...what controls the motion of celestial bodies through space? What is gravity in a globe model? Mainstream science says it's because of mass, density, and laws of physics. This is really no different in the enclosed world model. Mass and density would still apply, but there is also room for artificial systems to be used like molecular magnetism (magnets that can pull anything) which we have been using in simulations for years. These would be needed to affect things like the tides, because in this model, the moon isn't large enough to affect the oceans.

10.If the Earth is flat, why do certain types of TV/radio signals, the kind which do not propagate well through the atmosphere or reflect off the upper atmospheric layers, not penetrate farther than the horizon....the horizon calculated at the distance it would be on a round Earth? Several signals do not propagate well through atmospheric layers, but others travel much further than what we thought possible. A perfect example would be the US Navy 2 inch beam radar, which has been testified to paint targets at 60+ miles. Using the mainstream curve formula (see question 3 above) these ships should be thousands of feet BELOW the curvature, or "over the curved hill" as it were. These signals aren't bouncing off any layers, but are line of sight targeting. To hear testimonials from military personnel, please visit my YouTube channel.

11. If the Earth is flat, why can a very bright light such as a laser not be shone for hundreds or thousands of miles? Lasers are routinely bounced off the moon 240,000 miles away. Testing confirms that most scientific lasers disperse up to 2 feet every mile, which means that at 240 thousand miles, the beam would have spread to almost half a million feet. At that rate, there is no power left to have any reliable accuracy, let alone enough energy to bounce back to earth. Not to mention the moon reflector is claimed by NASA, the gatekeepers of the enclosed structure you live in. Search Flat Earth laser tests on YouTube and you will be surprised at what you find!

12. If the Earth is flat, why do distant objects disappear over the horizon? They don't, they just reach the vanishing point of your natural vision. There is some great footage online of boats that can't be seen with the naked eye, but become visible once the zoom is activated. Then they disappear past the limits of the zoom, and yet another camera can reacquire the ship. This isn't possible with what we are told about the curve.

13. If the Earth is flat, why does every picture of it from space look round? This question seems like the easiest, but will take some research on your part to confirm. From 1972, until July of 2015, there was exactly **ONE** picture of the full sunlit earth. This picture was supposedly taken during the return trip of Apollo 17, and no other picture was taken for 43 years, by any space program, **ever**. We know this because we the SECOND one was taken, the US white house tweeted about it: http://ecowatch.com/2015/07/21/obama-blue-marble-photo/

14. If the Earth is flat, how is it laid out? How do you reconcile travel distances between points in the northern and southern hemispheres, which make no

sense on a flat Earth? Why does no map of a flat Earth exist that is able to reconcile known distances? Currently, the best version of the Flat Earth Map is the Azimuthal Equidistant map, which is seen on the UN Flat. While this map appears to show the correct orientation of the continents, there are scale issues which are still being adjusting. It is true that Southern hemisphere flights become more direct using a flat map, some flights become problematic due to scale. There are some aspects to the continent layout that are still a mystery, but the community is working diligently to resolve it.

15. If the Earth is flat, what causes seasons? The seasons are caused by a combination of systems, not just the sun. In the enclosed model, the sun tracks over the top like a needle on a record player. As the song continues, the needle moves in towards the center. In this way the sun just marks the season. Yes, the sun gives off heat, but being that it is so much smaller, cannot generate everything that is needed for a full season change. There are two other structure systems which come into play. One is the jet stream, which in this model is just a very large air conditioning system, and the underwater conveyor, which circulates huge amounts of water around the disc. With these three, seasons are accommodated.

16. If the Earth is flat, what causes tides? A massive molecular magnet controls the tides, one that can move water. In this model the moon isn't large enough to control the tides. It also would be inefficient to use a direct magnetic force from such a small object over an area covering millions of square miles. Everything has to be controlled from below.

17. *If the Earth is flat, why are different stars seen in the Northern and Southern hemispheres? Surely everybody should see the same stars? Why do the stars move in exactly the same way they would if the Earth were, in fact, a ball?* Because the creators or architects of this place wanted to do exactly that, create the illusion of a globe. The stars are no different. We've been using programming technology to do this very sort of thing for the last 15 years. It's called using "instances" or the realization of objects. Or to put it simply, the visual creation of objects based on region. With it you can display multiple sets of stars, depending on where you are. You and your friend on the other side of the world think you're looking at the same thing, but in actuality, you are both seeing your own customized star, or moon, or planet. Ask any gamer, they'll confirm this.

18. *If the Earth is flat, and there is no gravity, what keeps its atmosphere from dissipating into space?* The enclosed structure is pressurized, which is why many in the FE movement prefer the dome model over a "convertible". Without a dome, force field, barrier, the vacuum of space would pull off the very air we need to breathe.

19. If the Earth is flat, where is the edge? Why has no one ever seen it? Why doesn't the ocean run off?
The edge of the world is the Antarctic coastline, which is much larger than we have been told for the last 100 years. It is also 200 feet high at the shoreline, and continues sharply in elevation up to 2 miles, then plateaus, more than high enough to hold any ocean in.

20. If the Earth is flat, why does traveling in a straight line not take planes and ships right to the edge? If you did have a way to travel exactly straight in any direction, you would reach the Antarctic coastline. The problem now is that your instruments have to rely on the GPS system, which was created 20 years ago by the US Department of Defense. That system will not let you fly exactly straight for that long. If you could bypass it and reach the Antarctic coastline, you would have other things to worry about, like the military, and no land markers as you continued on...

21. If the nature of the flat Earth is so obvious, why isn't there a single scientist, astronomer, or researcher who acknowledges such a thing? For the same reason the scientists who discovered it in 1956 weren't allowed to acknowledge it. If science is proven wrong on concept that they have been preaching for 500 years, then the entire academic community gets turned upside down, and more importantly, faith in science takes a huge nosedive. 99% of scientists today may know there is a problem with current world models and physics, but by the time you reach that education level, it's almost impossible to believe anything but the old theories. We're hoping to change that. Currently we've received testimonials from all branches of the US military and professionals related to this theory. The scientists are next.

22. Why can no flat Earth believer ever provide any real scientific explanation for their cosmological model with facts and figures to back it up? The burden of proof isn't on the Flat Earth community. It's on mainstream science, who, after a five century head start, should have MOUNTAINS of evidence on their side. One of the strengths in the FE movement is that they can quickly create doubt in astrophysics, astronomy, and of course NASA. It's like a court case. Look at all the things proposed by FE that create reasonable doubt in science. Now tell me who has the stronger case, and why FE has been able to do this in only one year.

23. *Why is there no flat Earth believer who can claim any scientific credentials whatsoever?* Science is in real trouble, and they know it. Remember, for almost 500 years the only "proof" that science had for the globe was math. Until you could get something high enough to take the picture, how could you be sure? Can we believe science, the same group that tells us what the earth core (and EVERY other planet) is made out of, even though they've drilled less than 1 percent down? No PHD in any physical science can switch sides on this, unless they are fully prepared to commit academic suicide. It's not impossible. Some of the testimonials we've received so far are well educated.

24. The earth is flat because there's 24 hour sunlight in the North Pole, and none of that in the southern tip of Argentina or South Africa, or even Australia. But only in the North Pole. How do the non-flat earthers explain this? We can't. The South Pole 24 hour sun is a mystery. It may be a technical feature that we haven't seen yet. Of course, it would help if all restrictions to Antarctica were lifted, so objective experiments could be done.

25. The heliocentric earth doesn't work, but the world isn't flat, it's concave! Light is bending in the concave earth. The light, and our sight curves more than earth, giving an illusion of a flat plane, illusion. The horizon will appear as flat because the horizon is where the curved light/sight meets your eye level. Ah yes, the concave argument, a distant cousin of the FE model. I actually don't hate the concave model, never have. They do however have one VERY big problem with their model, which is that if the ground slopes up, eventually we would see landscapes bending back on themselves, not to mention problems at night, seeing vertical cities in the dark, which we never do.

26. **How does this theory fit in with the hollow earth theory?** The Flat Earth theory doesn't conflict with the hollow earth theory. The models work quite well together. The hollow earth is just a cavernous region below ours that another civilization could live in. The entrances would still work around the FE model.

27. **What have NASA got to say about this?** NASA is surprisingly quiet during the last year in regards to Flat Earth, but they have revealed some amazing things recently. The first was the blue marble shot in June of 2015, followed by the Himiwari geostationary satellite which came on line the same month, followed by the moon transiting in front of another satellite, eventually leading to yet another lunar satellite releasing a composite image while flying over the moon surface. Combine that with a new space story almost every day, and I'd say they are reacting strongly to us, without saying anything.

28. **Once people start researching this, do they generally become convinced?** I'll let the numbers do the talking. In February of 2015, when I made the clues, you could type in "Flat Earth" into YouTube and get maybe 50,000 relevant hits. If you did the same search today, it comes in at 4,300,000. The reason is because this topic is so polarizing. No one is on the fence. You either love it or hate it. From what I've seen, if you dig into the research for even a few hours, you're hooked, and then it's like a marble inside a paint can. You can't get rid of it!

29. **What can't the flat earth explain? (What's the globalists' greatest argument?)** Not much. In fact, the only weakness we have right now is the map scale and the Antarctic 24 hour sun. These two things aren't nearly enough to overcome all the difficult questions that science can't answer.

30. **There are illuminati playing cards that mention the flat earth. Why has this topic 'all of a sudden' hit the internet? What are they really distracting us from?** That's the next question I'm going to be focusing on. The illuminati Flat Earth card was made decades ago, but is very telling. It feels to me that this whole concept is a setup for something even larger, if that's possible. If the FE is the left jab, then the right hook must be incredible!

Note – if you have any burning questions that aren't covered here, tune into **Strange World** at http://TruthFrequencyRadio.com currently aired on a Tuesday at 7:00PM Pacific Coast Time, USA – and ask your question there!

And as always... **do your own research!**

RESOURCES

Introduction

The USGS uses one of these maps, find it.
http://en.wikipedia.org/wiki/List_of_map_projections

High altitude nuclear testing
http://en.wikipedia.org/wiki/High-altitude_nuclear_explosion

The Flat Earth Society
http://www.theflatearthsociety.org/cms/

Definition of the Firmament
http://en.wikipedia.org/wiki/Firmament

Antarctic non colonization treaty
http://en.wikipedia.org/wiki/Antarctic_Treaty_System

The United Nations Flag
http://en.wikipedia.org/wiki/Flag_of_the_United_Nations

Clue One – The Empty Theatre

2001, A Space Odyssey, 1968 movie, shown before the
first moon mission -
https://en.wikipedia.org/wiki/2001:_A_Space_Odyssey#Film

Category: Films about the Apollo Program.
https://en.wikipedia.org/wiki/Category:Films_about_the_apoll
o_program

The Right Stuff, 1983 movie.
http://en.wikipedia.org/wiki/The_Right_Stuff_(film)

From the Earth to the Moon television series.
http://en.wikipedia.org/wiki/From_the_Earth_to_the_Moon_(T
V_miniseries)

Capricorn One 1978 movie.

http://en.wikipedia.org/wiki/Capricorn_One

Room 237 documentary.
http://en.wikipedia.org/wiki/Room_237

Clue Two – Admiral Byrd

US Television interview with Admiral Richard Byrd, 1954.
https://www.youtube.com/watch?v=czW0iRJuH1A

Antarctica, a land full of secrets.
http://en.wikipedia.org/wiki/Antarctica

Operation Highjump, a military operation against a hidden enemy.
http://en.wikipedia.org/wiki/Operation_Highjump

Operation Deep Freeze, the last public mission to Antarctica.
http://en.wikipedia.org/wiki/Operation_Deep_Freeze

Admiral Richard R. Byrd. Hero. Explorer. Legend.
http://en.wikipedia.org/wiki/Richard_E._Byrd

Longines Chronoscope, worst television show name ever.
http://en.wikipedia.org/wiki/Longines_Chronoscope

Clue Three – Map Makers

USGS, United States Geological Survey.
http://en.wikipedia.org/wiki/United_States_Geological_Survey

List of map projections.
https://en.wikipedia.org/wiki/List_of_map_projections

Flag of the United Nations.
https://en.wikipedia.org/wiki/Flag_of_the_United_Nations

Wiki FLAT EARTH
http://en.wikipedia.org/wiki/Flat_Earth

Al-Biruni, the origin of the AE map.

https://en.wikipedia.org/wiki/Al-Biruni

Al-Biruni (crater)
https://en.wikipedia.org/wiki/Al-Biruni_(crater)

Clue Four – Shell Beach

Dark City, 1998 movie.
http://en.wikipedia.org/wiki/Dark_City_(1998_film)

Truman Show, 1998 movie.
https://en.wikipedia.org/wiki/The_Truman_Show

The Village, 2004 movie.
https://en.wikipedia.org/wiki/The_Village_(2004_film)

1988 Twilight zone episode, basis for Truman show.
https://en.wikipedia.org/wiki/Special_Service

Reddit forum on logistical cost of Truman show.
https://www.reddit.com/r/theydidthemath/comments/1xyfa5/request_how_much_would_it_actually_cost_to/

Clue Five – Status Quo

The Firmament.
http://en.wikipedia.org/wiki/Firmament

Religion.
http://en.wikipedia.org/wiki/Religion

Richard E. Byrd.
http://en.wikipedia.org/wiki/Richard_E._Byrd

Clue Six – Depth Perception

The strange story of the world's deepest hole.
http://whenonearth.net/kola-superdeep-borehole-strange-story-worlds-deepest-hole/

Russian super deep drill hole:
http://en.wikipedia.org/wiki/Kola_Superdeep_Borehole

German super deep drill hole:
http://en.wikipedia.org/wiki/German_Continental_Deep_Drillin
g_Program

Scientific structure of the earth:
http://en.wikipedia.org/wiki/Structure_of_the_Earth

Clue Seven – The Long Haul

Travel Calculator
http://www.timeanddate.com/worldclock/distance.html

International Airports Australia.
http://www.infrastructure.gov.au/aviation/international/icao/d
esig_airports.aspx

International Airports New Zealand.
http://www.fourcorners.co.nz/new-zealand/international-
airports/

International Airports South America.
https://en.wikipedia.org/wiki/List_of_the_busiest_airports_in_
South_America

Commercial Airliner cruising speeds.
http://www.askcaptainlim.com/flying-the-plane-flying-90/645-
what-are-the-cruising-speeds-of-the-
various-airliners.html

The GPS System.
https://en.wikipedia.org/wiki/Global_Positioning_System

Clue Eight – Creative Force

World of Warcraft
http://us.battle.net/wow/en/character/stonemaul/Marksargent
/simple

Clue Nine – Magic Show

Planefinder.net
http://planefinder.net/

Examples of plane logs.
http://flightaware.com/live/flight/QFA27

http://uk.flightaware.com/live/flight/QFA27/history/20150228/0150Z/YSSY/SCEL/tracklog

http://uk.flightaware.com/live/flight/LAN800/history/20150227/0315Z/NZAA/SCEL/tracklog

Clue Eleven – Souls in the System

Astronauts Gone Wild
https://en.wikipedia.org/wiki/Astronauts_Gone_Wild

Red Light Camera
https://en.wikipedia.org/wiki/Red_light_camera

Clue Twelve – Realize

Maps – [Mercator and Gall Peters]
https://en.wikipedia.org/wiki/List_of_map_projections

Video of clue 12 -
https://www.youtube.com/watch?v=ditQ1BfwlRA

FAQ

The Pope and Flat Earth
https://youtu.be/KLnNa5KwkJo

B.o.B. – (Rapper) Flatline song
https://youtu.be/J3Oyad6IG1w

Connect Online

'Like' our page on FaceBook:
www.facebook.com/FlatEarthCluesBook

INDEX

ABOUT THE AUTHOR

Growing up on South Whidbey Island, Washington, Mark K Sargent started his career playing computer games professionally in Boulder Colorado. From there he spent the next 20 years training people in proprietary software. In 2014, he looked into what is no doubt the most ridiculous conspiracy ever, called "Flat Earth Theory", and through extensive research, discovered that it wasn't so laughable after all.

Early in 2015, he released a series of YouTube videos titled "Flat Earth Clues", which delves into the possibility of our human civilization actually being inside a "Truman show" like enclosed system, and how it's been hidden from the public since 1956. There is a Flat Earth Clues app on Android and iphone. Mark is a prepper. If he had to pick a motto it would be "Hope for the best. Prepare for the worst."

You can contact the author:
Email: msargent23@comcast.net
Phone: 303-494-6631
YouTube Channel: www.YouTube.com/MarkKSargent
Website: www.EnclosedWorld.com
Send cookies and fan mail to: 2410 James Place #502
Langley, WA 98260

ABOUT THE EDITOR IN CHIEF

Serial author Lisa Newton is a self-confessed conspiracy theorist who enjoys reading, writing and planning. In her spare time Lisa enjoys traveling, yoga, dancing salsa, learning languages and manifesting her cosmic orders.

A strong supporter of women in business and entrepreneurial people,
Lisa is an Ambassador for Enterprising Women (the UK campaign to give women confidence and ambition to be enterprising - to have ideas and to make them happen). She holds a first class honors degree in Accounting with Marketing and an MSc in Investment Management. She is a member of the ICB & the AAT.

Lisa is a serial entrepreneur and holds various directorships in various industries including telecoms, software, as well as finance. She has won various awards in Business including in 2015 AI (Accountancy International) award.

Lisa supports the charity The MS Society. A speaker, consultant and an avid net-worker, Lisa enjoys meeting people and working on projects with like-minded individuals. More about the Editor-in-Chief can be found at: **www.LisaNewton.co.uk**

ABOUT THE ILLUSTRATOR

Rosie Brooks was born in London. Winning a BBC Blue Peter poster competition at school launched a career and she soon began taking on professional commissions including for Comic Relief whilst at still at school.

Rosie studied Music at Durham University, designing wine and port labels for her college then went on to complete a Masters in Children's Book Illustration at the Ruskin School of Art, Cambridge where she was short listed for the Macmillan Children's Book Prize.

Since becoming a freelance Cartoonist and Illustrator Rosie has worked to build a long list of international credits. Her clients have ranged from Sir Paul McCartney to the Ministry of Education in Chile, A Suit that Fits (who paid her in a wardrobe of rather divine tailor made items), WaterAid, Ogilvy, M&C Saatchi, Pearson Education, and many, many more. Supported by the UKTI Rosie exhibits every year at the Bologna Children's Book Fair and is a regular contributor to the Campaign for Drawing's Big Draw events.

More about the Illustrator can be found at: **www.RosieBrooks.com**

You can contact the illustrator:
Email: rosie.brooks@gmail.com
Twitter: https://twitter.com/rosiebrookspics
Facebook: www.facebook.com/rosiebrooksillustrator

OTHER BOOKS (WHICH MAY BE OF INTEREST)

Cosmic Ordering With Vision Boards

Have you written long lists that just seem to gather dust? Fed up with 'wishing' and 'hoping' and not really 'having'? Still waiting on the dream job? Perfect match? More money? Author Lisa Newton can show you how a picture speaks 1000 words. Not just to you, but to the cosmos (who is always on standby, ready to deliver!) Allow thought vibration and visualization to align you to what you want. Newton can teach you how to make a Vision board, place your order and allow the receiving to come in. But be careful what you ask for, as you just might get it!

Author: Lisa Newton.
First Published: 2013
ISBN: 978-14921 13607

Order Form

To order any of these books please fill in the form below

No. of copies	Title	Price	Total
	Cosmic Ordering With Vision Boards	**£ 7.99**	
	Flat Earth Clues	**£ 8.95**	
	For P&P add £2.50 for the first book, £1 for each additional book		
	GRAND TOTAL		**£**

Name: _____

Address: _____

_____Postcode: _____

Daytime Tel. No./Email: _____

(In case of query)

AUDIOBOOK – NOTE: the audio version of this book is available from www.iTunes.com & www.Audible.com

'Like' the book on Facebook:
https://www.facebook.com/FlatEarthCluesBook

The Flat Earth Clues book page on the publishers site:
http://www.booglez.com/product/flat-earth-clues/

Four ways to pay:

1. Telephone the Booglez Hotline on **020 3371 8894**. Receptionists are there 24 hours a day, 7 days a week. And leave a message with them 'I'd like to order' and we'll call you back. Please have your card (debit or credit card handy).

2. I enclose a Cheque made payable to **Booglez** for £ _____

3. Please send a payment **via paypal** to info@booglez.com (or just email us and ask for a payment request)

4. Please charge my Visa [ ]   MasterCard [ ]   Amex [ ] Maestro (issue no. _____) [ ]

Card number: _ _ _ _ /_ _ _ _ / _ _ _ _ / _ _ _ _ / _ _ _

Expiry date: _ _ / _ _

Start date: _ _ / _ _

Last three digits on back of the card: _ _ _

Signature: _____

Please return forms to: (Photocopies acceptable)

**Direct Mail Dept., Booglez Books, 5th floor, 230 City Road, London, England EC1V 2TT, United Kingdom
Enquiries to: info@booglez.com**

Booglez (directly or via its agents) may mail, email or phone you about promotions or products.

[ ] Tick box if you do not want these from us

www.Booglez.com

Made in the USA
San Bernardino, CA
02 December 2016